AN INSIDE LOOK

THE ENVIRONMENT

For a free color catalog describing Gareth Stevens Publishing's list of high-quality books and multimedia programs, call 1-800-542-2595 (USA) or 1-800-461-9120 (Canada). Gareth Stevens Publishing's Fax: (414) 332-3567.

The editor would like to extend thanks to Keith A. Sverdrup, Associate Professor, Department of Geosciences, University of Wisconsin-Milwaukee, Milwaukee, Wisconsin, for his kind and professional help with the information in this book.

Library of Congress Cataloging-in-Publication Data available upon request from publisher. Fax: (414) 332-3567 for the attention of the Publishing Records Department.

ISBN 0-8368-2725-2

This North American edition first published in 2000 by
Gareth Stevens Publishing
A World Almanac Education Group Company
330 West Olive Street, Suite 100
Milwaukee, WI 53212 USA

This U.S. edition © 2000 by Gareth Stevens, Inc. Original edition © 1996 by Horus Editions Limited. First published as *The Environment* in the series *How It Works* by Horus Editions Limited, 1st Floor, 27 Longford Street, London NW1 3DZ, United Kingdom. Additional end matter © 2000 by Gareth Stevens, Inc.

Illustrators: Mike Saunders, Jim Channell, Gary Hincks, Ruth Lindsay, Brian Pearce, and David Wright
Gareth Stevens editors: Christy Steele and Heidi Sjostrom

Printed in Mexico

1 2 3 4 5 6 7 8 9 04 03 02 01 00

AN INSIDE LOOK

THE
ENVIRONMENT

Michael Allaby

Gareth Stevens Publishing
A WORLD ALMANAC EDUCATION GROUP COMPANY

AN INSIDE LOOK

CONTENTS

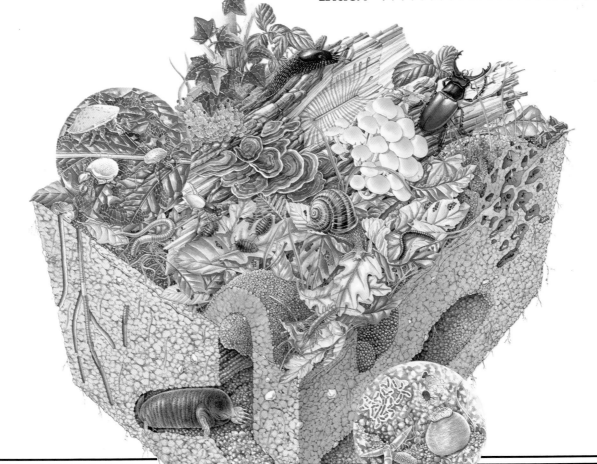

What Is the Environment?

Earth's environment is made up of all the natural systems on our planet. An environment is a place in which living organisms can find food and shelter. It consists of the surroundings, such as rocks, soil, air, and water, and the living organisms themselves. However, rather than looking at the environment as a whole, it is often easier to look at smaller parts of it. On Earth, life is possible almost everywhere, from the deepest ocean floor to dry land or the lower part of the atmosphere. Each of these places has its own unique surroundings and supports a special community of living organisms.

Mars and Venus are similar to Earth in many ways, but we are not sure that anything can live on these planets. An Earthlike environment must be created on these planets before humans can live there.

Planet Earth

Earth is made up of three layers. The two innermost layers are very hot and vary from 759 miles (1,221 kilometers) to 1,782 miles (2,867 km) in thickness. The core is the center layer of Earth. The inner core is made of hot, solid metal. This is surrounded by the outer core, which is made of molten metal. The mantle, a belt of huge rocks, is the middle layer of Earth. The soil and rock on which we live are called the crust — a layer only 3 to 37 miles (5 to 60 km) thick. The environment we live in is small compared to the rest of the planet beneath us. Above the crust, the atmosphere forms a thin, outer covering around Earth.

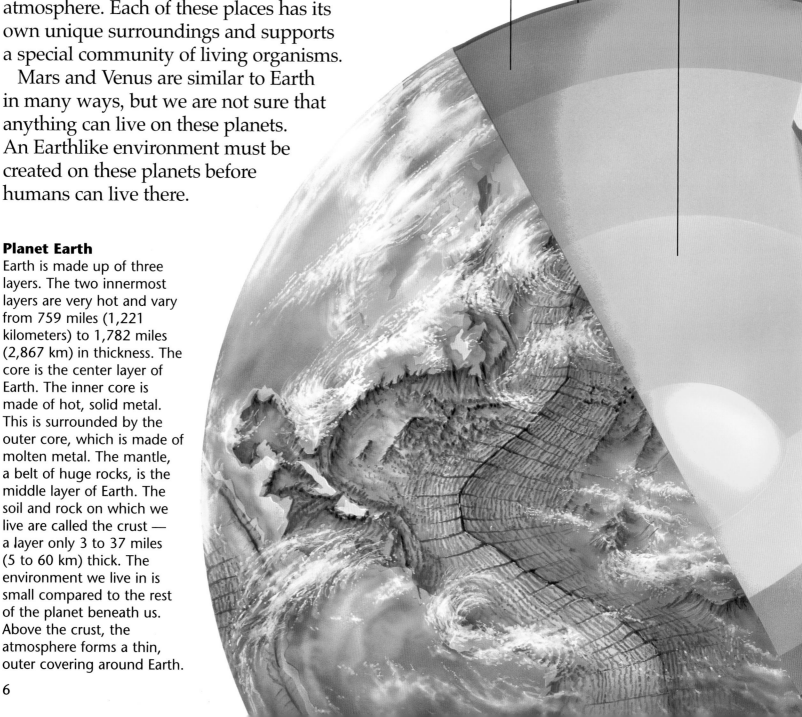

THE CRUST AND THE UPPER PART OF THE OUTER MANTLE ARE MADE OF LARGE PLATES THAT MOVE. THE MOVEMENT CAUSES CRACKS, RIDGES, AND MOUNTAINS TO FORM.

THE OUTER MANTLE CONTAINS MOLTEN ROCK THAT SOMETIMES ERUPTS FROM VOLCANOES.

REACHING 5.5 MILES (8.85 KM) HIGH, MOUNT EVEREST JUST REACHES THE STRATOSPHERE.

THE ENVIRONMENT STRETCHES FROM THE BOTTOM OF THE OCEANS TO THE TOP OF THE TROPOSPHERE.

THE OUTER CORE IS VERY HOT. ITS TEMPERATURE REACHES ABOUT 5,792° FAHRENHEIT (3,200° CELSIUS).

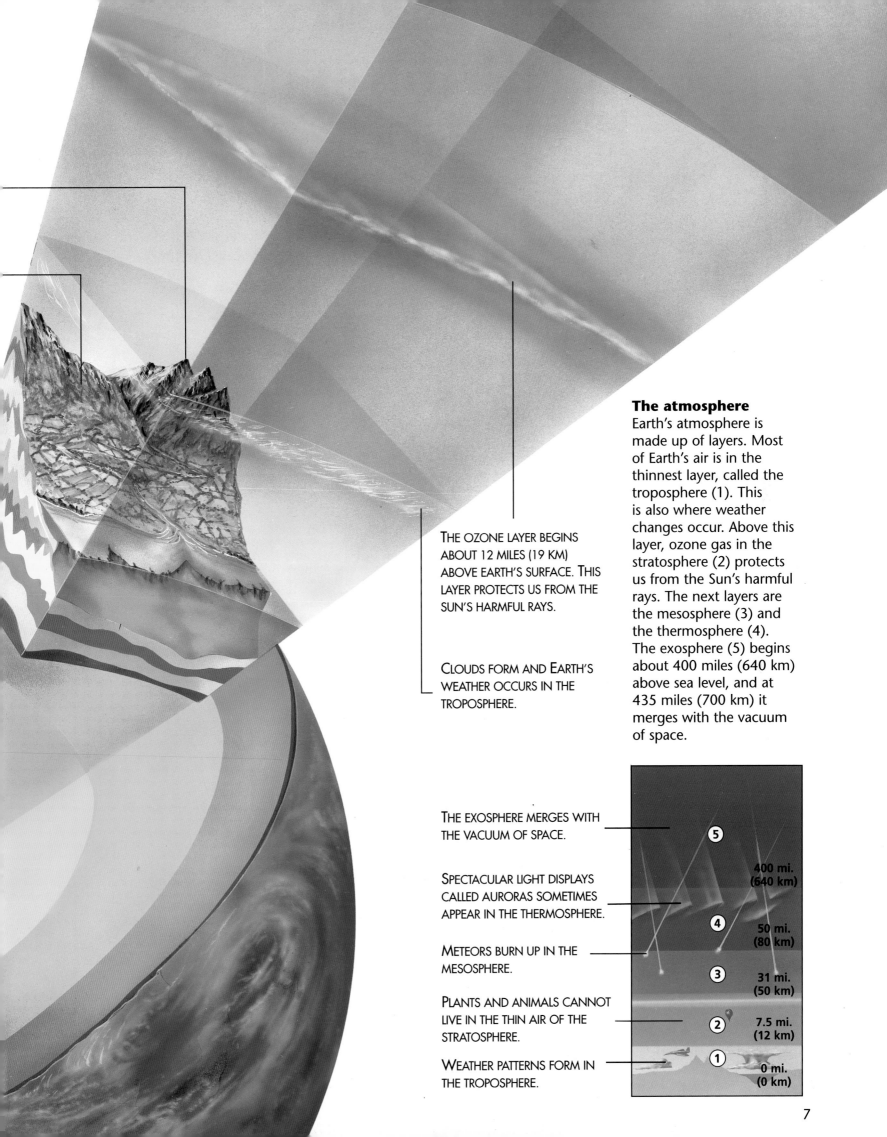

The atmosphere
Earth's atmosphere is made up of layers. Most of Earth's air is in the thinnest layer, called the troposphere (1). This is also where weather changes occur. Above this layer, ozone gas in the stratosphere (2) protects us from the Sun's harmful rays. The next layers are the mesosphere (3) and the thermosphere (4). The exosphere (5) begins about 400 miles (640 km) above sea level, and at 435 miles (700 km) it merges with the vacuum of space.

THE OZONE LAYER BEGINS ABOUT 12 MILES (19 KM) ABOVE EARTH'S SURFACE. THIS LAYER PROTECTS US FROM THE SUN'S HARMFUL RAYS.

CLOUDS FORM AND EARTH'S WEATHER OCCURS IN THE TROPOSPHERE.

THE EXOSPHERE MERGES WITH THE VACUUM OF SPACE.

SPECTACULAR LIGHT DISPLAYS CALLED AURORAS SOMETIMES APPEAR IN THE THERMOSPHERE.

METEORS BURN UP IN THE MESOSPHERE.

PLANTS AND ANIMALS CANNOT LIVE IN THE THIN AIR OF THE STRATOSPHERE.

WEATHER PATTERNS FORM IN THE TROPOSPHERE.

5

400 mi.
(640 km)

4

50 mi.
(80 km)

3

31 mi.
(50 km)

2

7.5 mi.
(12 km)

1

0 mi.
(0 km)

Climates and Currents

Air, water, and sunshine affect climate, weather, and the type of vegetation that grows in an environment. The Sun is almost directly over the equator at noon every day, so sunlight warms places on and near the equator more than it warms areas farther from the equator. Air that is heated by the Sun moves away from the equator. At the same time, cooler air moves in toward the equator. Earth's winds also help move air. The circulation of air creates weather changes. Warm and cold currents that flow through ocean water also affect climates because air is warmed or cooled as it passes over water.

Climate

Climate is the range of weather conditions found in a particular area. Generally, the farther an area is from the equator, the colder its climate. The climate of a region affects the type of vegetation found there. Rain forests (1) grow near the equator if the climate is both hot and wet. Deserts (2) are in very dry climates. Temperate forests (3) grow in mild climates, while evergreen forests (4) are often found in colder climates. Very little vegetation exists in polar regions (5) because the climate is dry and very cold.

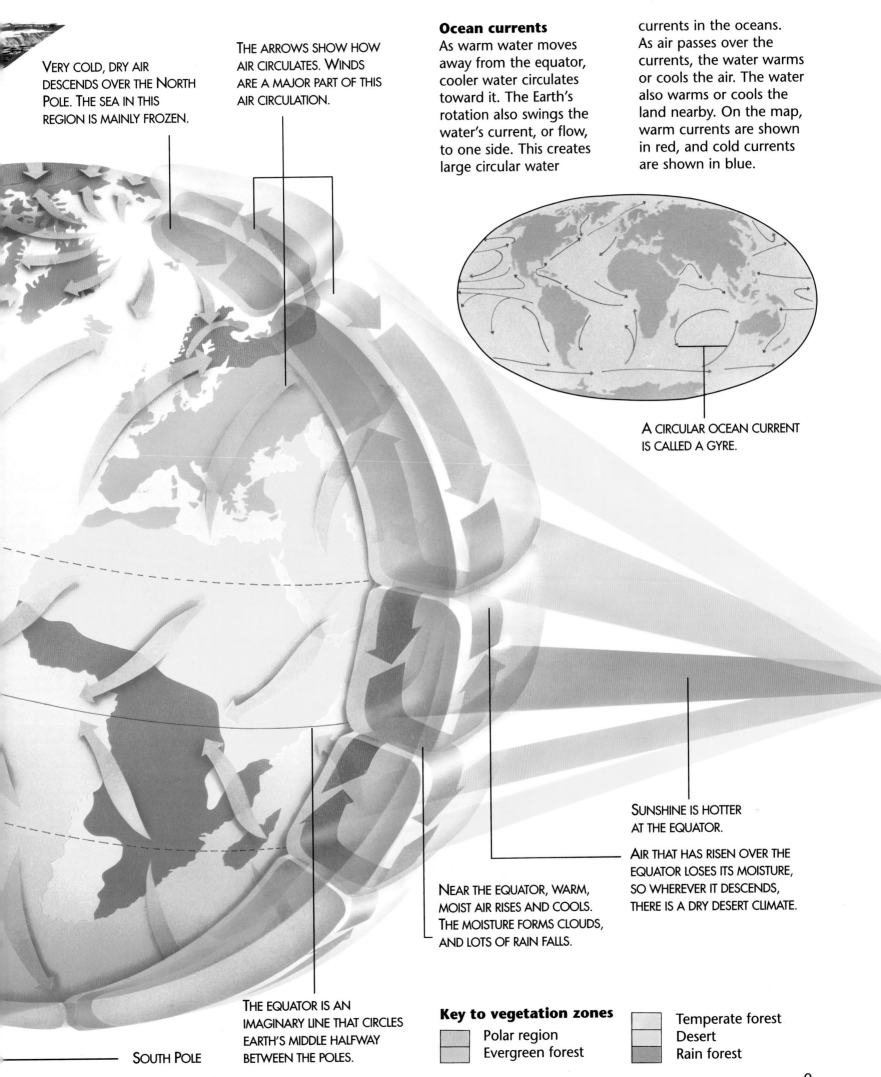

VERY COLD, DRY AIR DESCENDS OVER THE NORTH POLE. THE SEA IN THIS REGION IS MAINLY FROZEN.

THE ARROWS SHOW HOW AIR CIRCULATES. WINDS ARE A MAJOR PART OF THIS AIR CIRCULATION.

Ocean currents

As warm water moves away from the equator, cooler water circulates toward it. The Earth's rotation also swings the water's current, or flow, to one side. This creates large circular water currents in the oceans. As air passes over the currents, the water warms or cools the air. The water also warms or cools the land nearby. On the map, warm currents are shown in red, and cold currents are shown in blue.

A CIRCULAR OCEAN CURRENT IS CALLED A GYRE.

SUNSHINE IS HOTTER AT THE EQUATOR.

AIR THAT HAS RISEN OVER THE EQUATOR LOSES ITS MOISTURE, SO WHEREVER IT DESCENDS, THERE IS A DRY DESERT CLIMATE.

NEAR THE EQUATOR, WARM, MOIST AIR RISES AND COOLS. THE MOISTURE FORMS CLOUDS, AND LOTS OF RAIN FALLS.

THE EQUATOR IS AN IMAGINARY LINE THAT CIRCLES EARTH'S MIDDLE HALFWAY BETWEEN THE POLES.

SOUTH POLE

Key to vegetation zones

Polar region
Evergreen forest

Temperate forest
Desert
Rain forest

The Ozone Layer

The sun radiates, or gives off, different kinds of light. Sunlight may look white, but it is really a mixture of the colors in a rainbow. The Sun also radiates invisible light. Some of this light is called ultraviolet (UV) light. If too much UV light reaches Earth's surface, it can harm plants and animals and cause skin cancer.

A layer of ozone gas in the atmosphere protects us by absorbing some of the UV light. However, in some parts of the world, particularly over Antarctica, the ozone layer has become thinner, which allows more harmful UV light to reach Earth.

THE OZONE LAYER, WHERE OZONE GATHERS, IS 12 TO 30 MILES (19 TO 48 KM) ABOVE EARTH'S SURFACE.

AS UV LIGHT PASSES THROUGH THE OZONE LAYER, OZONE ABSORBS SOME OF IT.

A THINNING OF THE OZONE LAYER IS SOMETIMES DESCRIBED AS AN "OZONE HOLE."

WHERE THE OZONE LAYER IS THIN, MORE UV LIGHT REACHES EARTH'S SURFACE.

TOO MUCH UV LIGHT CAN CAUSE SERIOUS DAMAGE TO PLANTS AND ANIMALS.

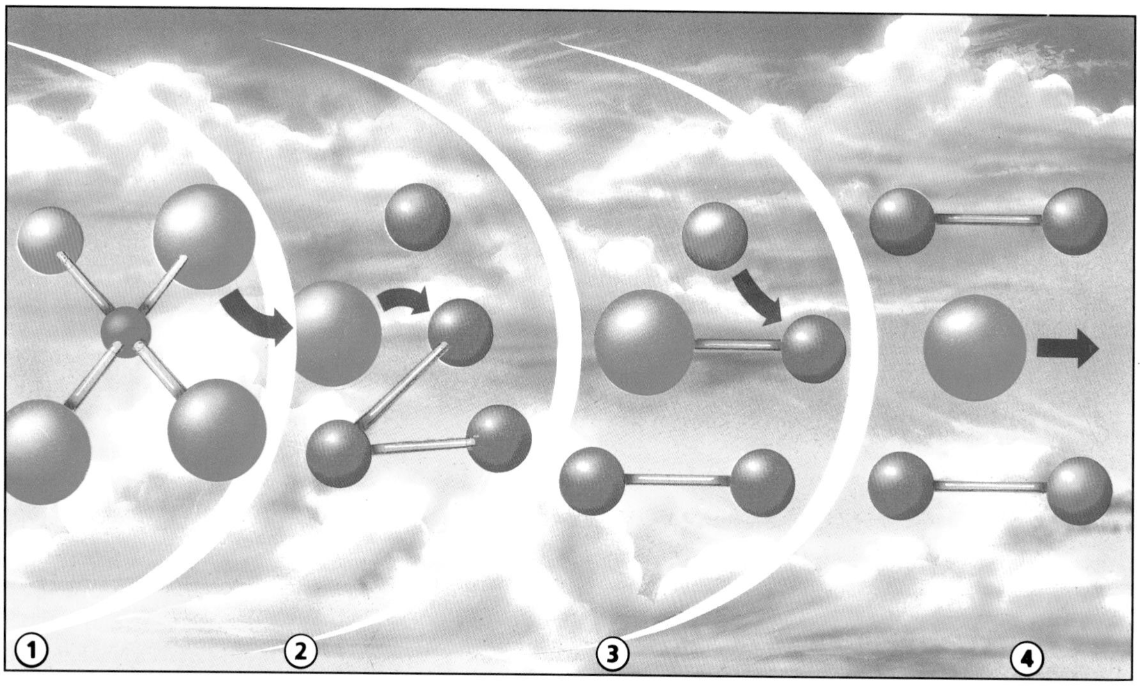

Ozone breakdown
Some gases in the ozone layer have chlorine atoms in their molecules. These gases include CFCs, or chlorofluorocarbons. A CFC molecule and its chlorine atoms are pictured above (1). The chlorine atoms are colored green. UV light from the Sun breaks apart these CFC molecules. The chlorine atoms break off and float away.

Over Antarctica, fierce winds blow around a center of still air during winter. Clouds of ice crystals form in the still air. On the surface of these crystals, the free chlorine atoms join to ozone molecules (2). This removes an oxygen atom (red) from the ozone molecule and breaks the molecule apart. The extra oxygen atom then leaves the chlorine to join

another oxygen atom (3). The chlorine is then free to break apart more ozone molecules (4). This eventually reduces the amount of ozone in the ozone layer and creates an ozone hole. Until recently, CFCs were widely used in items such as aerosol cans and refrigerators. Now that people know CFCs break apart ozone, their use is being stopped.

10

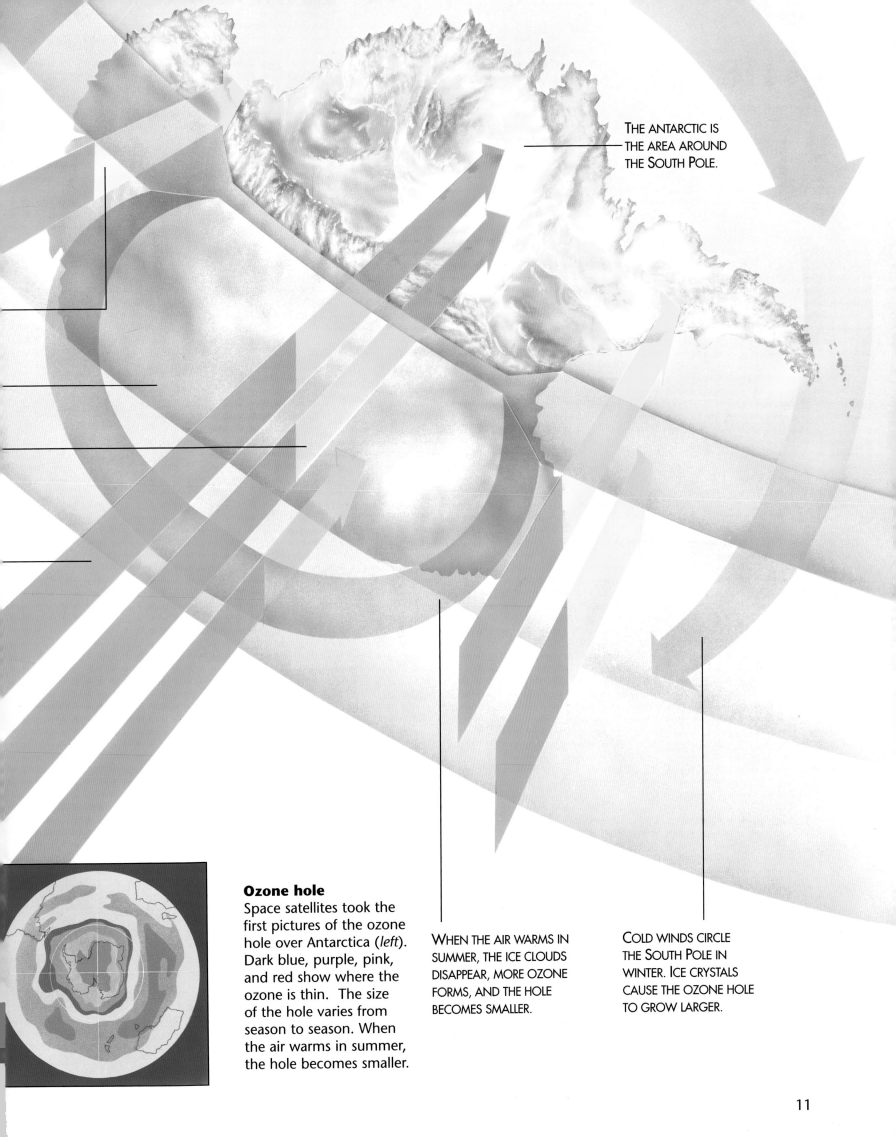

THE ANTARCTIC IS THE AREA AROUND THE SOUTH POLE.

Ozone hole
Space satellites took the first pictures of the ozone hole over Antarctica (*left*). Dark blue, purple, pink, and red show where the ozone is thin. The size of the hole varies from season to season. When the air warms in summer, the hole becomes smaller.

WHEN THE AIR WARMS IN SUMMER, THE ICE CLOUDS DISAPPEAR, MORE OZONE FORMS, AND THE HOLE BECOMES SMALLER.

COLD WINDS CIRCLE THE SOUTH POLE IN WINTER. ICE CRYSTALS CAUSE THE OZONE HOLE TO GROW LARGER.

The Greenhouse Effect

The Sun's rays pass through the air without warming it. However, when the Sun's rays reach land and water, these surfaces are warmed. The surfaces then send heat back up into the sky and the air becomes warm. The outgoing heat even warms some of the gases in the air. These "greenhouse" gases act like a blanket, holding in heat that would otherwise escape into space. This is called the greenhouse effect because, like the glass of a greenhouse, the gases allow heat energy to pass into Earth's atmosphere more easily than it can pass out of it.

THE AVERAGE TEMPERATURE OF EARTH'S SURFACE IS 59° FAHRENHEIT (15° C). WITHOUT THE GREENHOUSE EFFECT, IT WOULD BE -9.4° FAHRENHEIT (-23° C).

POWER STATIONS THAT BURN COAL OR NATURAL GAS EMIT GREENHOUSE GASES.

THE MOST IMPORTANT GREENHOUSE GAS IS CARBON DIOXIDE.

SOME SCIENTISTS BELIEVE THE RELEASE OF GREENHOUSE GASES BY INDUSTRIES SHOULD BE REDUCED, OR EARTH'S CLIMATE WILL GET HOTTER.

CARS BURN GASOLINE, RELEASING CARBON DIOXIDE AND NITROUS OXIDE, WHICH IS ANOTHER GREENHOUSE GAS.

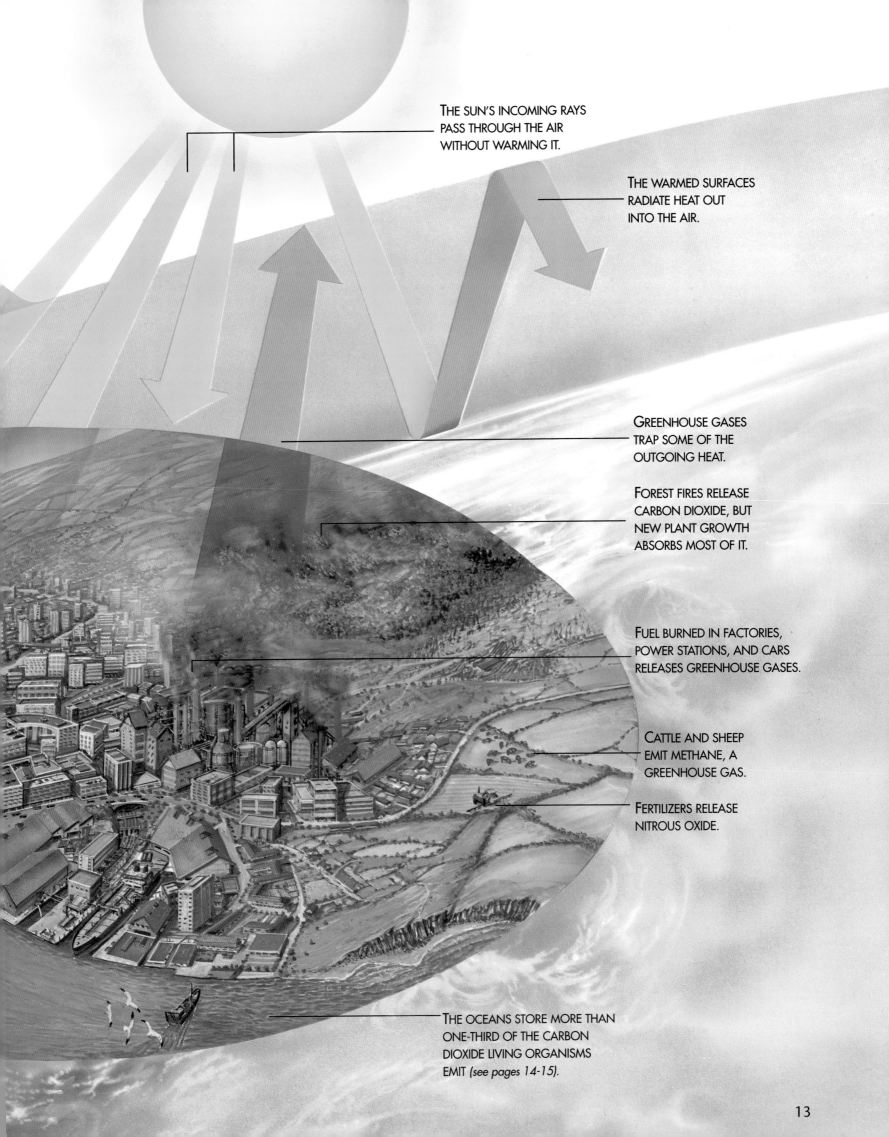

THE SUN'S INCOMING RAYS PASS THROUGH THE AIR WITHOUT WARMING IT.

THE WARMED SURFACES RADIATE HEAT OUT INTO THE AIR.

GREENHOUSE GASES TRAP SOME OF THE OUTGOING HEAT.

FOREST FIRES RELEASE CARBON DIOXIDE, BUT NEW PLANT GROWTH ABSORBS MOST OF IT.

FUEL BURNED IN FACTORIES, POWER STATIONS, AND CARS RELEASES GREENHOUSE GASES.

CATTLE AND SHEEP EMIT METHANE, A GREENHOUSE GAS.

FERTILIZERS RELEASE NITROUS OXIDE.

THE OCEANS STORE MORE THAN ONE-THIRD OF THE CARBON DIOXIDE LIVING ORGANISMS EMIT (see pages 14-15).

Gaia, The Living Earth

All living organisms change the chemistry of the environment. When we breathe, we remove oxygen from the air and add carbon dioxide to it. After digesting food, an organism's body rids itself of waste. These two events alone alter the environment.

In 1979, British scientist James Lovelock proposed the Gaia theory. According to the theory, on a "living" planet, organisms alter their environment. This, in turn, balances the environment. Lovelock explained that, in this way, Earth regulates itself, making sure, for example, that there is enough oxygen for animals to breathe and enough carbon dioxide for plants to make food. This diagram shows how small marine plants and shellfish regulate Earth's temperature and the amount of carbon dioxide (CO_2) in the air.

Carbon dioxide

Carbon dioxide is a greenhouse gas (see pages 12-13). It dissolves in rain, which falls into the sea. There, tiny plants and animals use it to make their calcium carbonate shells. When the organisms die, their shells fall to the seafloor. Eventually, these shells are ground down and form chalk and limestone rocks. These rocks are very common and often contain fossils of the shells.

This whole process removes carbon dioxide from the atmosphere and helps stop Earth from growing warmer. The average temperature on Earth has always been about 59° Fahrenheit (15° C).

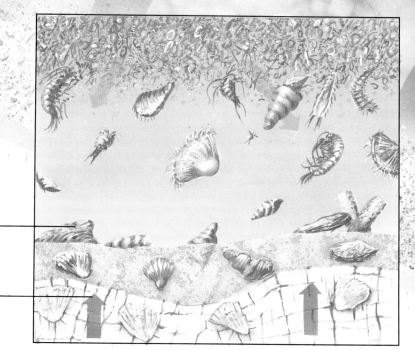

OVER MILLIONS OF YEARS, CHALK CLIFFS WERE FORMED BY DEAD MARINE ORGANISMS.

CHALK CLIFFS ARE LIKE GIANT STOREHOUSES FOR CO_2, WHICH IS STORED AS CALCIUM CARBONATE.

AS SHELLFISH AND SMALL ORGANISMS DIE AND BREAK APART, SOME CO_2 IS RELEASED IN THE WATER.

WHEN MARINE ORGANISMS DIE, THEIR BONES AND SHELLS MAKE A CHALKY SEDIMENT.

THE SEDIMENT BECOMES CHALK OR LIMESTONE ROCK, WHICH WILL KEEP GROWING UNTIL IT EVENTUALLY RISES ABOVE THE SEA'S SURFACE.

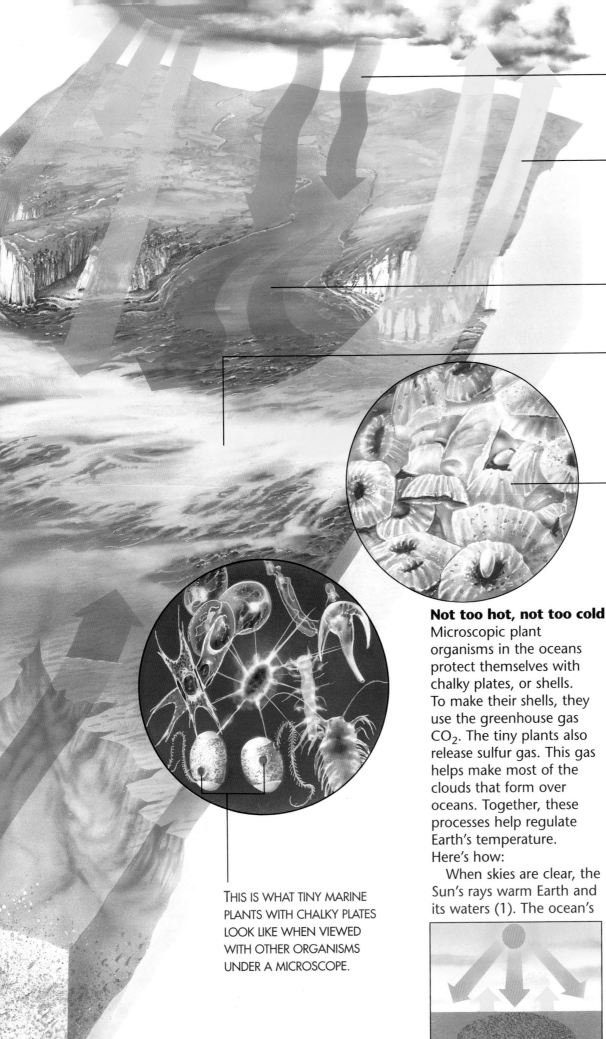

CO₂ FROM THE ATMOSPHERE DISSOLVES INTO RAIN. RAIN FALLS INTO RIVERS, WHICH CARRY THE CO₂ INTO THE SEA.

SULFUR IS RELEASED AS MARINE ORGANISMS GROW. THE SULFUR PRODUCES MORE CLOUDS AND MAKES TEMPERATURES FALL.

SEA ORGANISMS USE CO₂ TO MAKE THEIR BONES AND SHELLS.

MICROSCOPIC PLANTS CALLED PHYTOPLANKTON FLOAT IN SEAWATER. THEIR CHALKY SHELLS GIVE THE SEA A CREAMY APPEARANCE.

UNDER A MICROSCOPE, THE FOSSILS OF TINY MARINE PLANTS AND SHELLS CAN BE SEEN PRESERVED IN THE CHALK.

THIS IS WHAT TINY MARINE PLANTS WITH CHALKY PLATES LOOK LIKE WHEN VIEWED WITH OTHER ORGANISMS UNDER A MICROSCOPE.

Not too hot, not too cold

Microscopic plant organisms in the oceans protect themselves with chalky plates, or shells. To make their shells, they use the greenhouse gas CO_2. The tiny plants also release sulfur gas. This gas helps make most of the clouds that form over oceans. Together, these processes help regulate Earth's temperature. Here's how:

When skies are clear, the Sun's rays warm Earth and its waters (1). The ocean's tiny plants then multiply faster and remove more CO_2 from the air. The multiplying plants also release more sulfur, which makes clouds form. Clouds block sunlight, and the ocean surface cools (2). As the water temperature cools, the tiny plants begin to die. As they decompose, the plants release CO_2 back into the air. The amount of sulfur is reduced, the skies clear, the ocean warms up, and the entire cycle will begin all over again.

① ②

Plant Life

Plants are among the few living organisms on Earth that can make their own food. They make food through a process called photosynthesis. Sunlight falling on a plant's leaves is captured by chlorophyll, the substance in the plant's cells that gives the plant its green color. Energy from the light is used to combine water and carbon dioxide to make food in the form of sugars. This food is then transported to all the other parts of the plant and provides the energy the plant needs to live and grow. The plant also uses energy to take needed minerals from the soil to build its cells. The by-product of photosynthesis is oxygen, which passes out of the plant through its leaves.

SUNLIGHT FALLS ON THE PLANT'S GREEN LEAVES.

CHLOROPHYLL IN THE LEAVES CAPTURES THE SUNLIGHT.

IN PHOTOSYNTHESIS, OXYGEN IS RELEASED INTO THE SURROUNDING ATMOSPHERE.

LEAVES ARE GREEN BECAUSE THEY CONTAIN CHLOROPHYLL.

WATER TRAVELS UP VESSELS, OR TUBES, IN THE STEM.

WATER AND NUTRIENTS TAKEN FROM THE SOIL ENTER THE PLANT THROUGH ITS ROOTS.

CARBON DIOXIDE FROM THE ATMOSPHERE ENTERS THROUGH STOMATA IN THE LEAVES.

Respiration
Both plants and animals continuously respire, or breathe. Almost like reversed photosynthesis, respiration is when plants take in oxygen and release carbon dioxide. Plants use oxygen to break down the sugars they make and produce the energy they need to live.

During the day, photosynthesis occurs faster than respiration, so plants take in more carbon dioxide than they release. At night, photosynthesis stops, and plants no longer take in carbon dioxide. Instead, carbon dioxide is released as a respiration by-product.

CARBON DIOXIDE, OXYGEN, AND WATER VAPOR PASS THROUGH STOMATA.

AT NIGHT, PLANTS RELEASE ONLY RESPIRATION BY-PRODUCTS, WHICH ARE CARBON DIOXIDE AND WATER VAPOR.

UPPER EPIDERMIS

LOWER EPIDERMIS

WATER TRAVELS THROUGH THESE TUBES.

PHOTOSYNTHESIS TAKES PLACE IN CHLOROPHYLL INSIDE THE CYLINDRICAL CELLS.

SUGARS ARE STORED IN THE MESOPHYLL LAYER.

SUNLIGHT IS CAPTURED IN THE PALISADE LAYER.

Inside the leaf
This highly-magnified cross-section of a leaf shows the cells where photosynthesis takes place. Water vapor, oxygen, and carbon dioxide enter and leave through stomata, the tiny holes found mainly on the leaf's lower surface. Sunlight is taken in by chlorophyll in cylindrical cells in the palisade layer. Sugars made during photosynthesis are stored in the spongy mesophyll layer before transportation to other parts of the plant.

Food Webs

Green plants make their own food (*see pages 16-17*). They are the first in a line of organisms, along which food energy is passed. This line is called a food chain. Plants, the primary producers, are the first link in the chain. The second link is plant-eating animals. They are primary consumers. Meat-eating animals, called carnivores, are at the top of the food chain. They are secondary consumers.

In a plant and animal community, many food chains exist, and many are connected. When scientists link each food to the animal that eats it, they create a food web, such as the one illustrated here.

Food chains
Most food chains begin with green plants. Plant-eaters, such as rabbits, eat plants. Nine-tenths of the energy in the food is used up by a rabbit's digesting the food, moving, and keeping warm or cool. Therefore, a fox that eats a rabbit gets only the one-tenth of the rabbit's food energy that was left to build tissue. This energy loss can be shown as a pyramid.

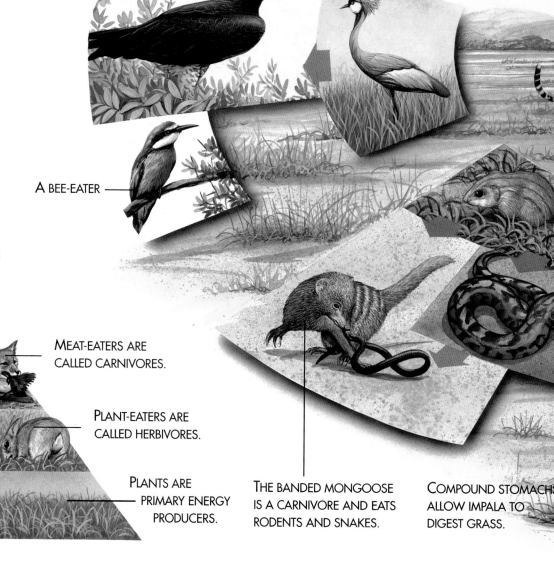

HYENAS CAN CRUSH LARGE BONES WITH THEIR STRONG JAWS AND TEETH.

VULTURES ARE SCAVENGERS, FEEDING ON ANIMAL REMAINS LEFT BEHIND BY THE HUNTERS.

MARTIAL EAGLES HUNT MAMMALS AND LARGE BIRDS.

A BEE-EATER

ONLY ONE-TENTH OF WHAT A RABBIT EATS BECOMES BODY TISSUE.

MEAT-EATERS ARE CALLED CARNIVORES.

PLANT-EATERS ARE CALLED HERBIVORES.

PLANTS ARE PRIMARY ENERGY PRODUCERS.

THE BANDED MONGOOSE IS A CARNIVORE AND EATS RODENTS AND SNAKES.

COMPOUND STOMACHS ALLOW IMPALA TO DIGEST GRASS.

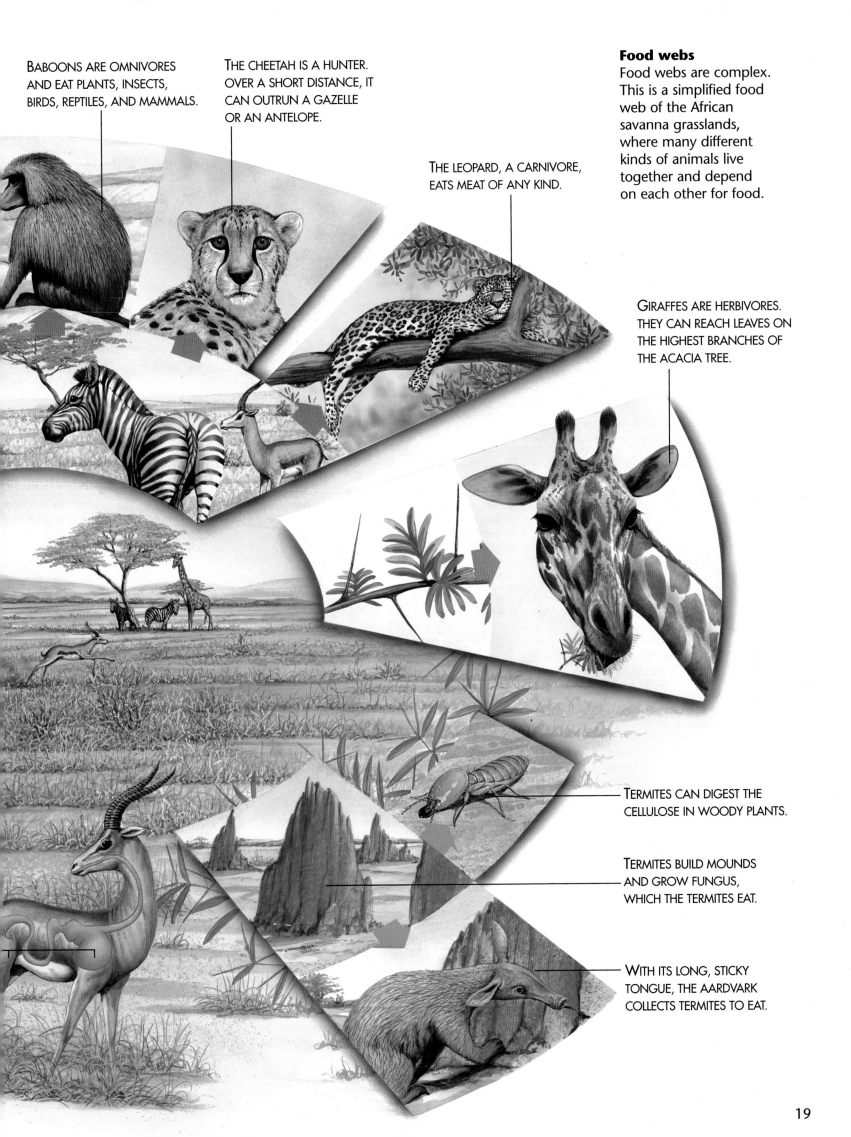

BABOONS ARE OMNIVORES AND EAT PLANTS, INSECTS, BIRDS, REPTILES, AND MAMMALS.

THE CHEETAH IS A HUNTER. OVER A SHORT DISTANCE, IT CAN OUTRUN A GAZELLE OR AN ANTELOPE.

THE LEOPARD, A CARNIVORE, EATS MEAT OF ANY KIND.

Food webs
Food webs are complex. This is a simplified food web of the African savanna grasslands, where many different kinds of animals live together and depend on each other for food.

GIRAFFES ARE HERBIVORES. THEY CAN REACH LEAVES ON THE HIGHEST BRANCHES OF THE ACACIA TREE.

TERMITES CAN DIGEST THE CELLULOSE IN WOODY PLANTS.

TERMITES BUILD MOUNDS AND GROW FUNGUS, WHICH THE TERMITES EAT.

WITH ITS LONG, STICKY TONGUE, THE AARDVARK COLLECTS TERMITES TO EAT.

The Living Oceans

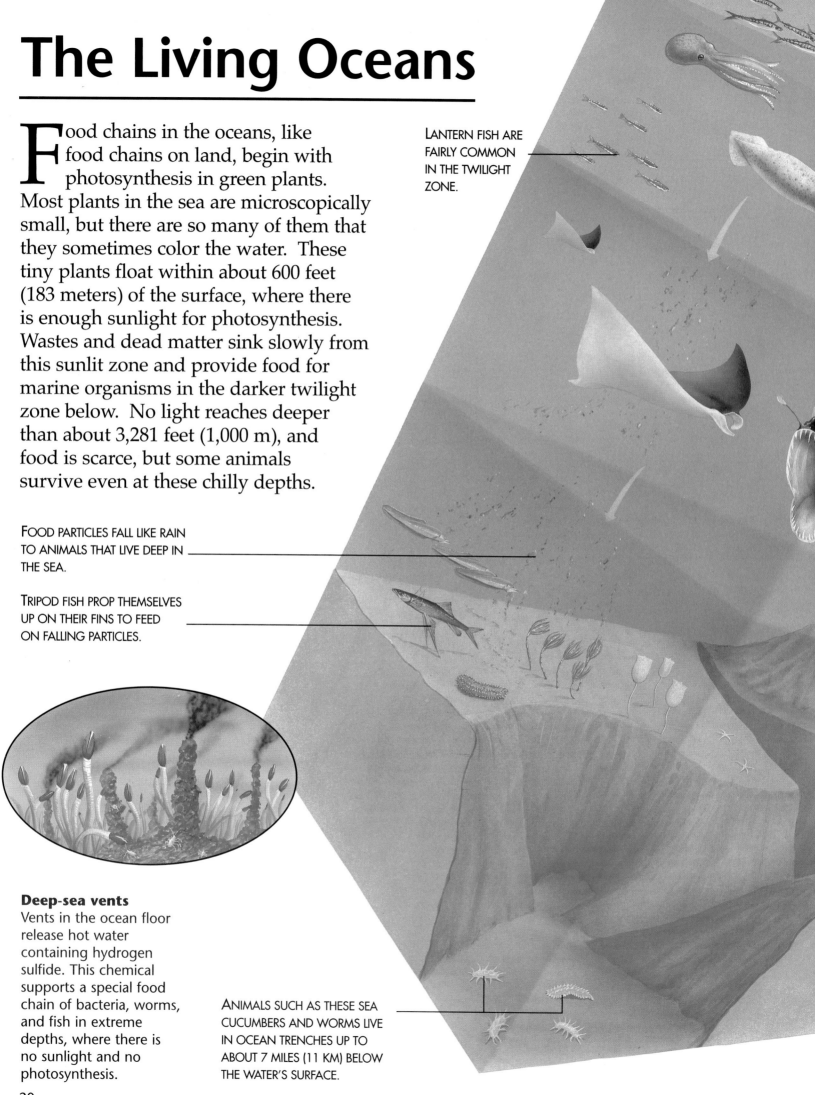

ood chains in the oceans, like food chains on land, begin with photosynthesis in green plants. Most plants in the sea are microscopically small, but there are so many of them that they sometimes color the water. These tiny plants float within about 600 feet (183 meters) of the surface, where there is enough sunlight for photosynthesis. Wastes and dead matter sink slowly from this sunlit zone and provide food for marine organisms in the darker twilight zone below. No light reaches deeper than about 3,281 feet (1,000 m), and food is scarce, but some animals survive even at these chilly depths.

LANTERN FISH ARE FAIRLY COMMON IN THE TWILIGHT ZONE.

FOOD PARTICLES FALL LIKE RAIN TO ANIMALS THAT LIVE DEEP IN THE SEA.

TRIPOD FISH PROP THEMSELVES UP ON THEIR FINS TO FEED ON FALLING PARTICLES.

Deep-sea vents
Vents in the ocean floor release hot water containing hydrogen sulfide. This chemical supports a special food chain of bacteria, worms, and fish in extreme depths, where there is no sunlight and no photosynthesis.

ANIMALS SUCH AS THESE SEA CUCUMBERS AND WORMS LIVE IN OCEAN TRENCHES UP TO ABOUT 7 MILES (11 KM) BELOW THE WATER'S SURFACE.

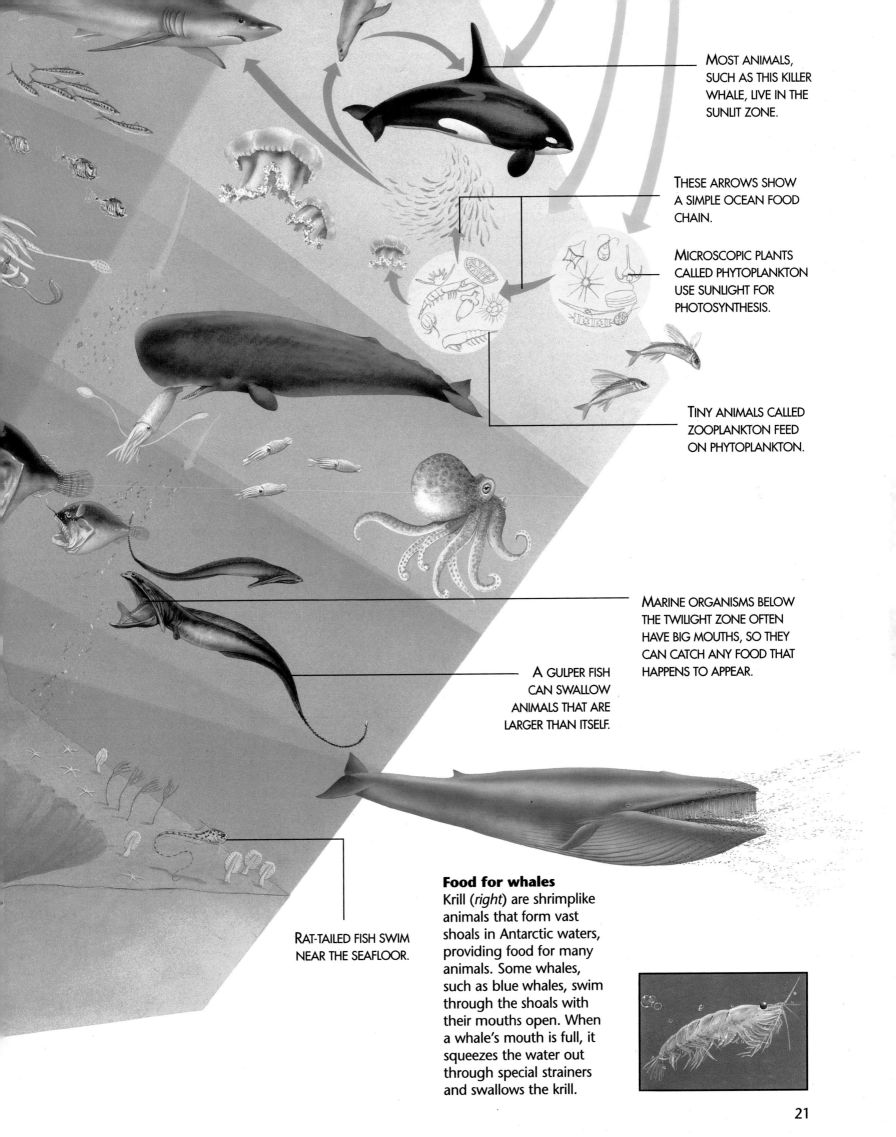

MOST ANIMALS, SUCH AS THIS KILLER WHALE, LIVE IN THE SUNLIT ZONE.

THESE ARROWS SHOW A SIMPLE OCEAN FOOD CHAIN.

MICROSCOPIC PLANTS CALLED PHYTOPLANKTON USE SUNLIGHT FOR PHOTOSYNTHESIS.

TINY ANIMALS CALLED ZOOPLANKTON FEED ON PHYTOPLANKTON.

MARINE ORGANISMS BELOW THE TWILIGHT ZONE OFTEN HAVE BIG MOUTHS, SO THEY CAN CATCH ANY FOOD THAT HAPPENS TO APPEAR.

A GULPER FISH CAN SWALLOW ANIMALS THAT ARE LARGER THAN ITSELF.

RAT-TAILED FISH SWIM NEAR THE SEAFLOOR.

Food for whales

Krill (*right*) are shrimplike animals that form vast shoals in Antarctic waters, providing food for many animals. Some whales, such as blue whales, swim through the shoals with their mouths open. When a whale's mouth is full, it squeezes the water out through special strainers and swallows the krill.

Migration

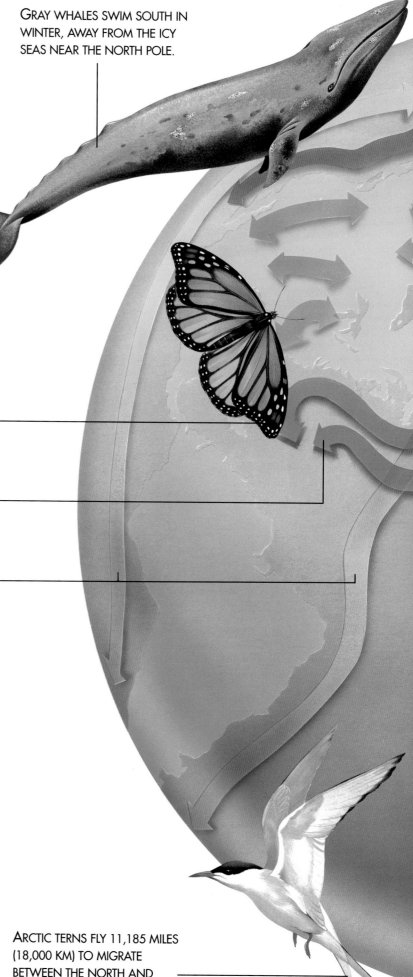

GRAY WHALES SWIM SOUTH IN WINTER, AWAY FROM THE ICY SEAS NEAR THE NORTH POLE.

Except for regions near the equator, most climates on Earth are seasonal. This means that part of the year is too dry or too cold for plants to grow. However, animals must eat whether plants are growing or not. Animals must also make sure that their young are born in the right place and at the right time. This way, the parents will be able to find enough food to feed their young. Many animals avoid difficult seasons by migrating, or regularly moving to another place. Each year, when their food supply begins to run out, these animals make journeys, some of which are very long.

EACH SPRING AND AUTUMN, MONARCH BUTTERFLIES FLY NEARLY 1,864 MILES (3,000 KM).

EELS MIGRATE TO THE SARGASSO SEA.

THE LONGEST MIGRATION IS THAT OF THE ARCTIC TERN. TWICE A YEAR, THIS BIRD FLIES NONSTOP FOR FOUR MONTHS.

Key to migration routes
- monarch butterfly
- gray whale
- caribou
- eel
- European swallow
- wildebeest
- Arctic tern

Seasons
Earth takes a year to orbit the Sun and a day to turn on its own axis. This axis is not at right angles to the Sun's rays, so as Earth orbits, first one hemisphere and then the other is tilted toward the Sun. This produces the seasons. The hemisphere tilted toward the Sun experiences summer, while the other hemisphere has its winter.

HERE IT IS SUMMER IN THE NORTHERN HEMISPHERE.

HERE IT IS SUMMER IN THE SOUTHERN HEMISPHERE.

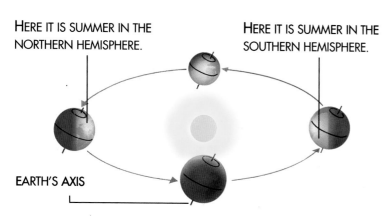

EARTH'S AXIS

ARCTIC TERNS FLY 11,185 MILES (18,000 KM) TO MIGRATE BETWEEN THE NORTH AND SOUTH POLES.

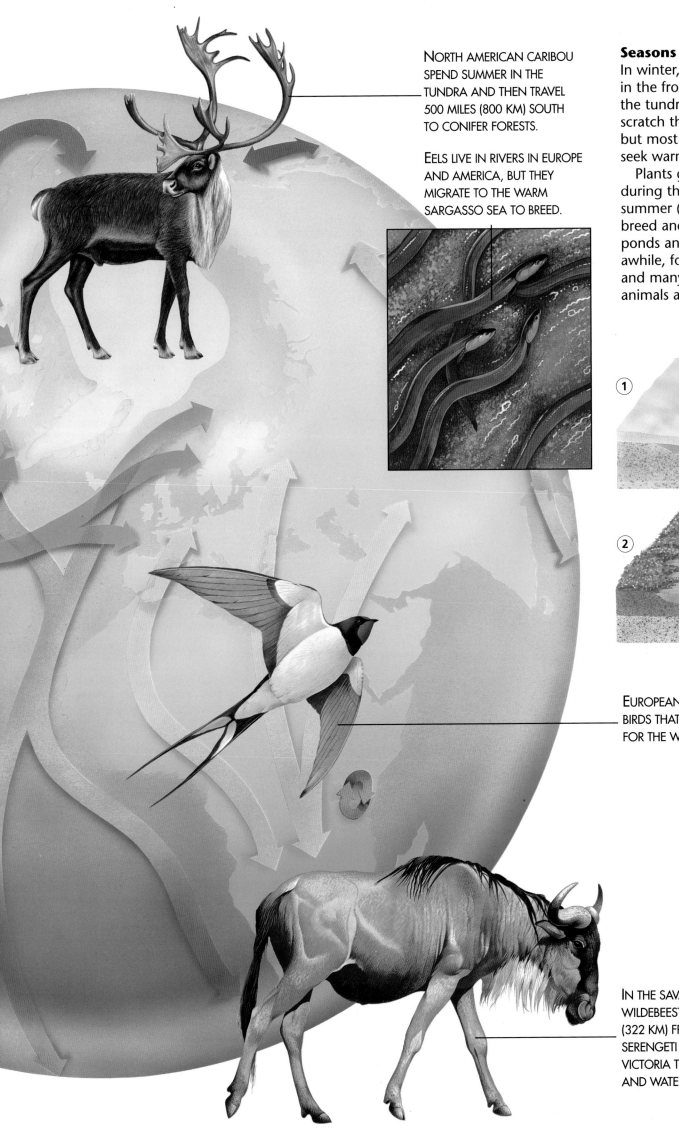

NORTH AMERICAN CARIBOU SPEND SUMMER IN THE TUNDRA AND THEN TRAVEL 500 MILES (800 KM) SOUTH TO CONIFER FORESTS.

EELS LIVE IN RIVERS IN EUROPE AND AMERICA, BUT THEY MIGRATE TO THE WARM SARGASSO SEA TO BREED.

Seasons and the tundra

In winter, there is little food in the frozen lands called the tundra (1). Reindeer scratch through the snow, but most animals leave to seek warmer conditions.

Plants grow rapidly during the tundra's brief summer (2). Insects, too, breed and swarm in the ponds and marshes. For awhile, food is plentiful, and many birds and animals arrive to feed.

①

②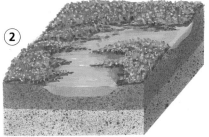

EUROPEAN SWALLOWS ARE BIRDS THAT MIGRATE TO AFRICA FOR THE WINTER.

IN THE SAVANNA DRY SEASON, WILDEBEEST TRAVEL 200 MILES (322 KM) FROM THE DRY SERENGETI PLAIN TO LAKE VICTORIA TO FIND FOOD AND WATER.

Niches

Every animal has a special role to play and a specific place to live within the larger community of living things. This is the animal's unique niche. Organisms will create niches for themselves wherever there is anything to eat and wherever there is shelter or enough space. No place in the environment stays empty long. Something will come to that habitat to live and create a niche for itself. The new arrival may be a plant, an animal, or a colony of bacteria.

For example, moss, a plant, may begin to grow on a stone that has been on the ground for a long time. The stone meets the needs of the moss. It can attach itself firmly on the rock. It obtains the nutrients it needs from the stone and gets enough water from the moist air or rain. The moss has found its niche. In doing so, it also provides niches for others, including the small animals that feed on it. Hundreds of niches may exist on a single oak tree (*right*).

HUNDREDS OF NICHES FOR OTHER PLANTS AND ANIMALS EXIST ON ONE OAK TREE.

THE CUCKOO IS A BROOD PARASITE; IT USES OTHER BIRDS TO RAISE ITS YOUNG. HERE, IT IS THROWING OUT A BLACKBIRD'S EGG TO MAKE ROOM FOR ITS OWN EGG IN THE NEST.

THE WOODPECKER'S NEST

A WOODPECKER DRILLS INTO THE BARK TO FIND INSECTS.

THIS MOTH'S MARKINGS MAKE IT ALMOST INVISIBLE ON A PATCH OF LICHEN.

LICHENS, FUNGI, AND FERNS USE THE TREE'S BRANCHES AND TRUNK FOR SUPPORT.

SQUIRRELS EAT ACORNS AND BUILD NESTS HIGH ABOVE THE GROUND, WHERE THEY CAN STAY SAFE.

BANK VOLES FIND FOOD AND SHELTER IN THE GRASS AROUND TREE ROOTS.

IN SPRING, CATERPILLARS FEED ON THE TREE'S LEAVES.

A niche for a beetle
An oak tree shelters and feeds many insects and their young. For example, the grubs of longhorn beetles eat the wood, drilling tunnels as they chew. If too many grubs feed on a tree, the tree can be seriously harmed.

BATS MAY ROOST IN HOLES IN THE TREE.

A TAWNY OWL RESTS ON THE TREE, WATCHING AND LISTENING FOR ITS PREY.

MANY SONGBIRDS, SUCH AS THIS BLACKBIRD, SLEEP AND BUILD NESTS IN BRANCHES.

PLANT LIFE USES FOOD AND WATER THAT COLLECTS IN HOLLOWS AND CREVICES IN THE TREE'S BARK.

Urban niche
Foxes eat almost anything and are always ready to try something new. Many of them visit towns, and some live there all the time, feeding on scraps thrown out by people. They find shelter in parks and gardens, and they find food in garbage cans. Since they have food and shelter, foxes have made niches for themselves near people's homes.

SOME TINY WASPS MAKE THE TREE GROW GALLS, IN WHICH THEY SHELTER THEIR YOUNG.

The Life Cycle of a Lake

An area of land can go through many changes. For example, a lake can become dry land, and dry land may eventually become woodland. At each stage, a different group of plants and animals arrives to live there.

These pages show how a community of living things has occupied a lake and its shores. We can also see the gradual buildup of mud and dead material on the lake bottom. These are signs that the lake will eventually become dry land. New plants are growing in the buildup of mud on the shoreline, and insects and birds are finding shelter in the new plant growth.

PLANTS LIKE CATTAILS GROW IN MUD THAT IS WASHED INTO THE LAKE BY RAIN OR CARRIED THERE BY A RIVER.

THE LAKE BECOMES MORE SHALLOW AS MUD COLLECTS ON ITS BOTTOM.

SOME PLANTS FLOAT ON THE LAKE'S SURFACE.

WATER LILIES ARE ROOTED IN THE LAKE BED, AND THEIR LEAVES FLOAT ON THE SURFACE.

DEAD PLANTS SINK TO THE LAKE BOTTOM.

LAKES FORM IN PLACES WHERE ROCK STOPS WATER FROM DRAINING DOWNWARD.

THE LAKE IS ALSO HOME TO FISH, SUCH AS THIS BREAM (ABOVE) AND PIKE (RIGHT).

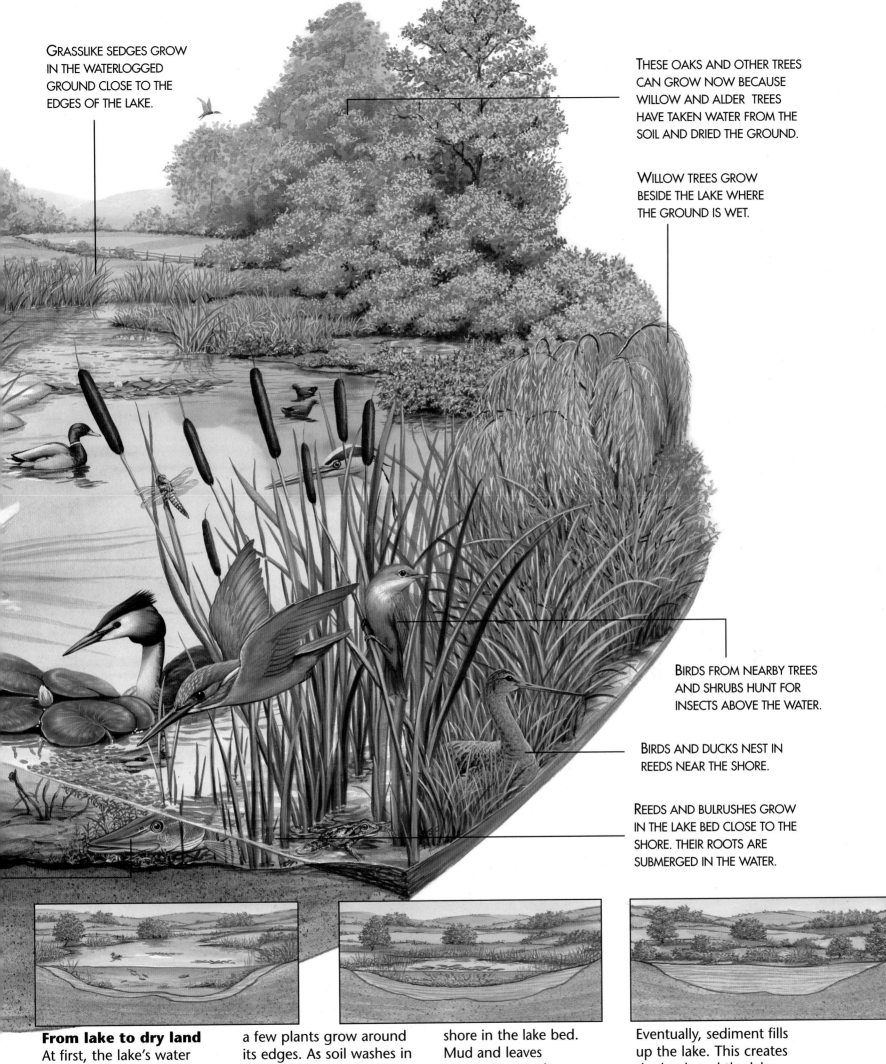

GRASSLIKE SEDGES GROW IN THE WATERLOGGED GROUND CLOSE TO THE EDGES OF THE LAKE.

THESE OAKS AND OTHER TREES CAN GROW NOW BECAUSE WILLOW AND ALDER TREES HAVE TAKEN WATER FROM THE SOIL AND DRIED THE GROUND.

WILLOW TREES GROW BESIDE THE LAKE WHERE THE GROUND IS WET.

BIRDS FROM NEARBY TREES AND SHRUBS HUNT FOR INSECTS ABOVE THE WATER.

BIRDS AND DUCKS NEST IN REEDS NEAR THE SHORE.

REEDS AND BULRUSHES GROW IN THE LAKE BED CLOSE TO THE SHORE. THEIR ROOTS ARE SUBMERGED IN THE WATER.

From lake to dry land
At first, the lake's water does not contain much food for plants, so just a few plants grow around its edges. As soil washes in from nearby land, plants take root farther from the shore in the lake bed. Mud and leaves accumulate, and more plants take root. Eventually, sediment fills up the lake. This creates dry land, and the lake ceases to exist.

Ecosystems

An ecosystem is a community of plants and animals living and interacting with each other and the physical surroundings. If one community is different from others nearby, it can be studied by itself as an ecosystem.

Tropical rain forests are very rich ecosystems. They grow near the equator where the climate is hot and wet. They can support many more kinds of plants and animals than cooler climates can. Plants grow rapidly because there are no cold or dry seasons to interrupt their growth. These diagrams show how rain forests provide countless niches and many small ecosystems within the main forest ecosystem.

A CACIQUE BUILDS ITS NEST IN THE CANOPY.

EMERGENTS ARE TREES THAT STAND HIGHER THAN THE OTHER TREES.

THE TAMANDUA AND SLOTH LIVE IN THE TREETOPS, CALLED THE CANOPY, WHERE MORE FOOD, SUCH AS FRUIT AND INSECTS, CAN BE FOUND.

YOUNG TREES FORM A LOWER CANOPY.

EPIPHYTES ARE PLANTS, OFTEN ROOTLESS, THAT PERCH ON TREES. THIS BROMELIAD IS AN EPIPHYTE.

LIANAS, OR WOODY VINES, ARE CLIMBERS THAT WIND AROUND TREES AS THEY GROW UPWARD TOWARD THE LIGHT. THEY HANG LIKE ROPES FROM TREE BRANCHES.

SAPLINGS AND SHRUBS GROW IN THE SHADY UNDERSTORY.

A JAGUAR HUNTS FOR PREY ON THE DARK FOREST FLOOR.

RAIN FORESTS CONTAIN MANY INSECTS. THESE ARMY ANTS ARE FINDING FOOD.

SPREADING BUTTRESS ROOTS GROW ABOVE THE GROUND AND SUPPORT THE HUGE TREES.

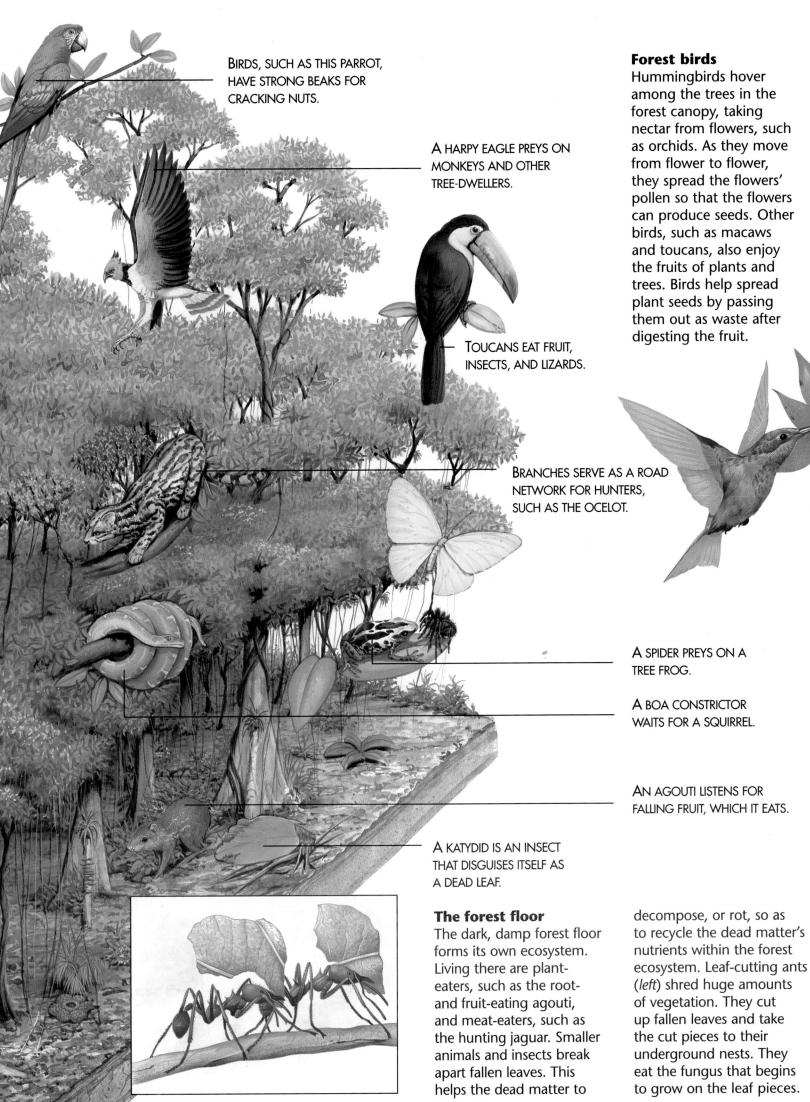

BIRDS, SUCH AS THIS PARROT, HAVE STRONG BEAKS FOR CRACKING NUTS.

A HARPY EAGLE PREYS ON MONKEYS AND OTHER TREE-DWELLERS.

TOUCANS EAT FRUIT, INSECTS, AND LIZARDS.

BRANCHES SERVE AS A ROAD NETWORK FOR HUNTERS, SUCH AS THE OCELOT.

A SPIDER PREYS ON A TREE FROG.

A BOA CONSTRICTOR WAITS FOR A SQUIRREL.

AN AGOUTI LISTENS FOR FALLING FRUIT, WHICH IT EATS.

A KATYDID IS AN INSECT THAT DISGUISES ITSELF AS A DEAD LEAF.

Forest birds

Hummingbirds hover among the trees in the forest canopy, taking nectar from flowers, such as orchids. As they move from flower to flower, they spread the flowers' pollen so that the flowers can produce seeds. Other birds, such as macaws and toucans, also enjoy the fruits of plants and trees. Birds help spread plant seeds by passing them out as waste after digesting the fruit.

The forest floor

The dark, damp forest floor forms its own ecosystem. Living there are plant-eaters, such as the root- and fruit-eating agouti, and meat-eaters, such as the hunting jaguar. Smaller animals and insects break apart fallen leaves. This helps the dead matter to decompose, or rot, so as to recycle the dead matter's nutrients within the forest ecosystem. Leaf-cutting ants (*left*) shred huge amounts of vegetation. They cut up fallen leaves and take the cut pieces to their underground nests. They eat the fungus that begins to grow on the leaf pieces.

29

Biomes

When one type of ecosystem covers a vast area, it is called a biome. Different climates produce different biomes. Africa contains several biomes, including tropical rain forests, savanna grasslands, and deserts. An African desert biome, such as the Sahara, forms in hot areas where there is little rain. There are extreme temperature ranges in a desert biome; it can be freezing at night after being very hot during the day. Savanna grasslands border the Sahara Desert. The savanna is also warm and dry, but, unlike the desert, it receives heavy rains in late spring.

Key to biomes map

- mixed forest
- mountain
- grassland
- tropical rain forest
- semi-desert
- desert

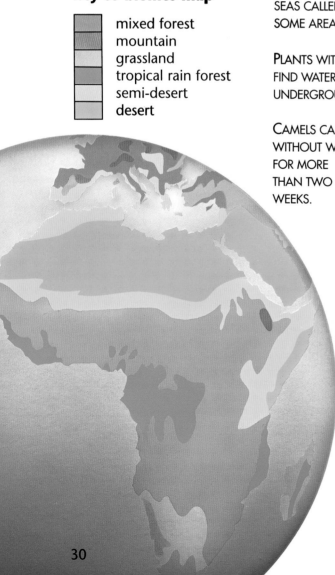

IN THE SAHARA, DAYTIME TEMPERATURES ARE AROUND 104° FAHRENHEIT (40° C).

PARTS OF THE SAHARA RECEIVE LESS THAN 2 INCHES (5 CENTIMETERS) OF RAIN A YEAR.

SAND STORMS OCCUR WHEN STRONG WINDS LIFT DUST AND SAND HIGH INTO THE AIR.

FENNEC FOX

JERBOA

THE SAHARA HAS VAST SAND SEAS CALLED ERGS, BUT IN SOME AREAS IT IS ROCKY.

PLANTS WITH LONG ROOTS FIND WATER DEEP UNDERGROUND.

CAMELS CAN SURVIVE WITHOUT WATER FOR MORE THAN TWO WEEKS.

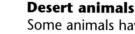

DESERT SOIL IS THIN.

Desert animals
Some animals have adapted to the desert climate. Lizards and jerboas take shelter from the heat in burrows. The fennec fox and jerboa (*see above*) have large ears with many blood veins to help them release body heat. The ostrich gets water from eating juicy plants and animals, and it can tolerate high body temperatures.

FROM 20 TO 71 INCHES (50 TO 180 CM) OF RAIN FALLS EACH YEAR IN THE SAVANNA.

GRASSLAND FIRES ARE COMMON IN THE DRY SEASON.

THE SAVANNA HAS DAYTIME TEMPERATURES AROUND 68° FAHRENHEIT (20° C).

After the fire
Fires are common in the dry savanna. Plants and trees are destroyed, but seeds survive because they lie hidden deep in the soil. The topsoil's nutrients are enriched by ash from fires and by decomposed plant remains.

Grassland grazers
Grazing animals live in large herds. Each type of animal prefers different plants, so they do not fight over food. In the dry season, when water is scarce, animals meet at water holes. Elephants, wildebeest, zebras, giraffes, and others drink or wallow together peacefully. However, the animals must remain alert because the water hole also attracts hunters, such as lions, leopards, cheetahs, and hyenas. Some grassland animals, such as the impala, get all of their water from dew-soaked grass, so they do not need to drink at water holes.

SEEDS SURVIVE BELOW THE SOIL.

AS THE DRY SEASON APPROACHES, MIXED HERDS OF GRAZERS MIGRATE TO FIND FRESH PASTURE.

TREES LIKE THE BAOBAB RESIST DROUGHT AND GROW RAPIDLY DURING THE RAINY SEASON.

ELEPHANTS GATHER TO DRINK AND BATHE AT THE WATER HOLE.

THE SAVANNA IS A REGION OF TALL GRASSES AND SCATTERED TREES THAT ARE GREEN ONLY WHEN IT RAINS.

WATER HOLES FORM IN HOLLOWS WHERE UNDERGROUND WATER SEEPS TO THE SURFACE.

SAVANNA SOIL IS DEEPER THAN DESERT SOIL.

Nutrient Cycles

All living organisms, including people, are made of about twenty chemical elements, such as carbon, nitrogen, calcium, and sulfur. Plants and animals use these nutrients to build their cells and to provide themselves with energy. Therefore, plants and animals must regularly ingest these chemicals. Nutrients come from an organism's environment. Plants absorb mineral nutrients, such as sulfur and calcium, with water from the soil. They absorb carbon from the air. Animals take in nutrients by eating plants or other animals.

Special cycles in Earth's environment help organisms reuse nutrients. The cycles return nutrients to the environment to allow new living things to live and grow. If nutrient chemicals did not get recycled, soon there would be none left, and all life would cease.

The sulfur cycle
This large illustration shows how sulfur follows a cycle. Sulfur is taken from rocks by plants and passes to animals that eat the plants. Animal wastes and dead animal and plant matter decompose, returning sulfur to the ground. It is then carried away by groundwater and rivers to the sea. Some sulfur is trapped in mud in estuaries. There, bacteria release a different form of sulfur back into the air.

Most of the sulfur is taken in by tiny sea plants called phytoplankton. These marine organisms also release another form of the sulfur back into the air. Sulfur in the air eventually falls back to the ground in rain.

Volcanoes bring up extra sulfur from beneath Earth's crust and release it into the air. In this way, they return to the sulfur cycle some of the sulfur that is trapped deep underground.

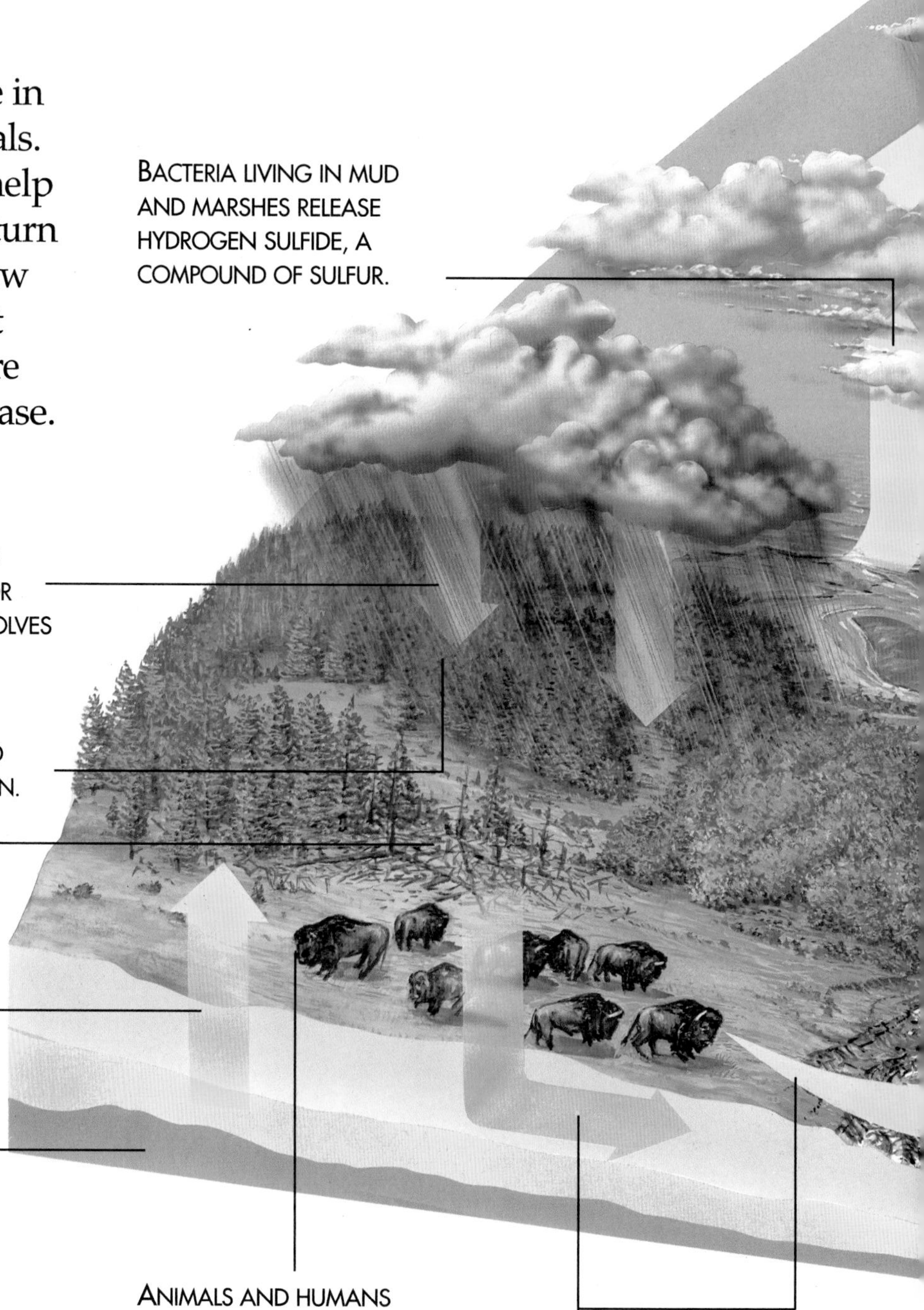

BACTERIA LIVING IN MUD AND MARSHES RELEASE HYDROGEN SULFIDE, A COMPOUND OF SULFUR.

SULFUR, IN VARIOUS CHEMICAL FORMS OR COMPOUNDS, DISSOLVES INTO RAINDROPS.

SULFUR IS RETURNED TO THE LAND IN RAIN.

NUTRIENTS FROM DEAD PLANTS AND ANIMALS ARE RELEASED BACK INTO THE GROUND THROUGH DECOMPOSITION.

SULFUR IS TAKEN IN BY LIVING PLANTS AND ANIMALS.

SULFUR ORIGINALLY COMES FROM ROCKS.

ANIMALS AND HUMANS NEED SULFUR TO MAKE PROTEINS. SKIN AND HAIR CONTAIN SULFUR.

GROUNDWATER AND RIVERS TAKE SULFUR TO THE SEA.

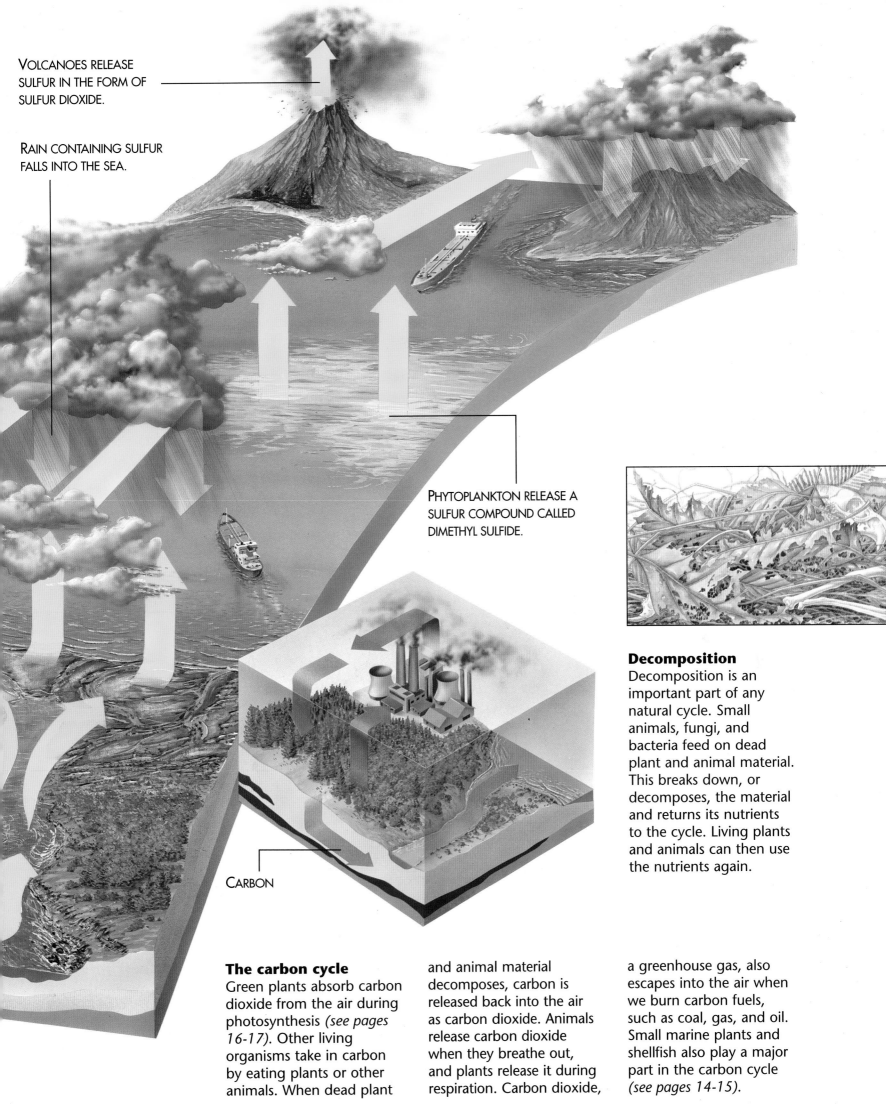

VOLCANOES RELEASE SULFUR IN THE FORM OF SULFUR DIOXIDE.

RAIN CONTAINING SULFUR FALLS INTO THE SEA.

PHYTOPLANKTON RELEASE A SULFUR COMPOUND CALLED DIMETHYL SULFIDE.

CARBON

Decomposition

Decomposition is an important part of any natural cycle. Small animals, fungi, and bacteria feed on dead plant and animal material. This breaks down, or decomposes, the material and returns its nutrients to the cycle. Living plants and animals can then use the nutrients again.

The carbon cycle

Green plants absorb carbon dioxide from the air during photosynthesis *(see pages 16-17)*. Other living organisms take in carbon by eating plants or other animals. When dead plant and animal material decomposes, carbon is released back into the air as carbon dioxide. Animals release carbon dioxide when they breathe out, and plants release it during respiration. Carbon dioxide, a greenhouse gas, also escapes into the air when we burn carbon fuels, such as coal, gas, and oil. Small marine plants and shellfish also play a major part in the carbon cycle *(see pages 14-15)*.

33

Obtaining Nitrogen

A nutrient cycle involves many complicated chemical changes. This is especially true of the nitrogen cycle. Although plenty of nitrogen exists in the air, plants and animals cannot use nitrogen in a gas form. They must have it in the form of food. This means that nitrogen gas has to be changed into nitrogen compounds, such as nitrates. Nitrogen-fixing bacteria in the soil perform this complicated chemistry. These bacteria change nitrogen into nitrates, which plants can then use to make proteins, the chemical "building blocks" of which plant and animal bodies are made. Animals take in nitrates when they eat plants. Then animal and plant waste recycles the nitrogen.

AIR IS MADE UP MOSTLY OF NITROGEN GAS.

ENERGY FROM LIGHTNING CHANGES NITROGEN GAS INTO A COMPOUND THAT DISSOLVES IN WATER.

NITROGEN COMPOUNDS FALL TO THE SOIL IN RAINWATER.

NITRATES IN WATER ENTER PLANT ROOTS AND FEED THE PLANT.

The nitrogen cycle
Nitrates that are dissolved in water are drawn up from the soil through the roots of plants. Plants use the nitrates to make proteins. Animals that eat plants change plant proteins into animal proteins.

Animal and plant wastes contain proteins and other nitrogen compounds. When these wastes decompose, the nitrogen compounds are once more available to plants. Some bacteria in soil, called denitrifying bacteria (right), break apart nitrogen compounds and release nitrogen gas back into the air.

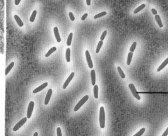

DENITRIFYING BACTERIA

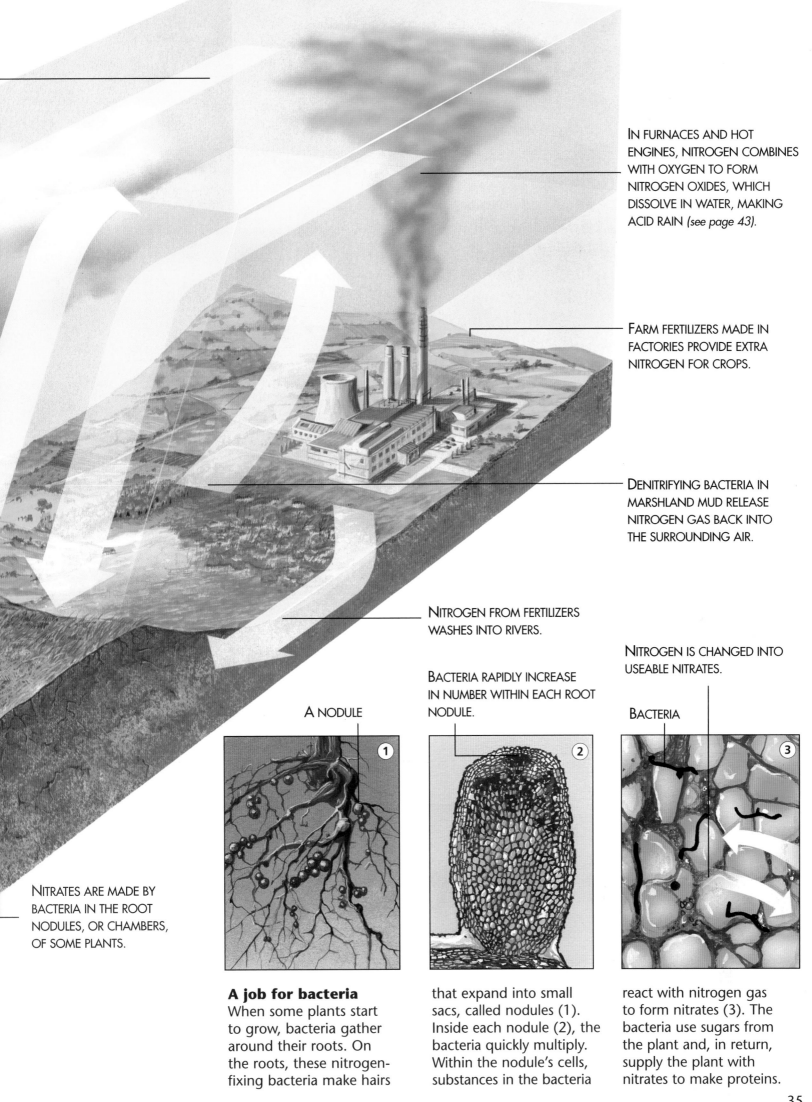

IN FURNACES AND HOT ENGINES, NITROGEN COMBINES WITH OXYGEN TO FORM NITROGEN OXIDES, WHICH DISSOLVE IN WATER, MAKING ACID RAIN *(see page 43)*.

FARM FERTILIZERS MADE IN FACTORIES PROVIDE EXTRA NITROGEN FOR CROPS.

DENITRIFYING BACTERIA IN MARSHLAND MUD RELEASE NITROGEN GAS BACK INTO THE SURROUNDING AIR.

NITROGEN FROM FERTILIZERS WASHES INTO RIVERS.

NITROGEN IS CHANGED INTO USEABLE NITRATES.

BACTERIA RAPIDLY INCREASE IN NUMBER WITHIN EACH ROOT NODULE.

BACTERIA

A NODULE

NITRATES ARE MADE BY BACTERIA IN THE ROOT NODULES, OR CHAMBERS, OF SOME PLANTS.

A job for bacteria
When some plants start to grow, bacteria gather around their roots. On the roots, these nitrogen-fixing bacteria make hairs that expand into small sacs, called nodules (1). Inside each nodule (2), the bacteria quickly multiply. Within the nodule's cells, substances in the bacteria react with nitrogen gas to form nitrates (3). The bacteria use sugars from the plant and, in return, supply the plant with nitrates to make proteins.

35

Soil

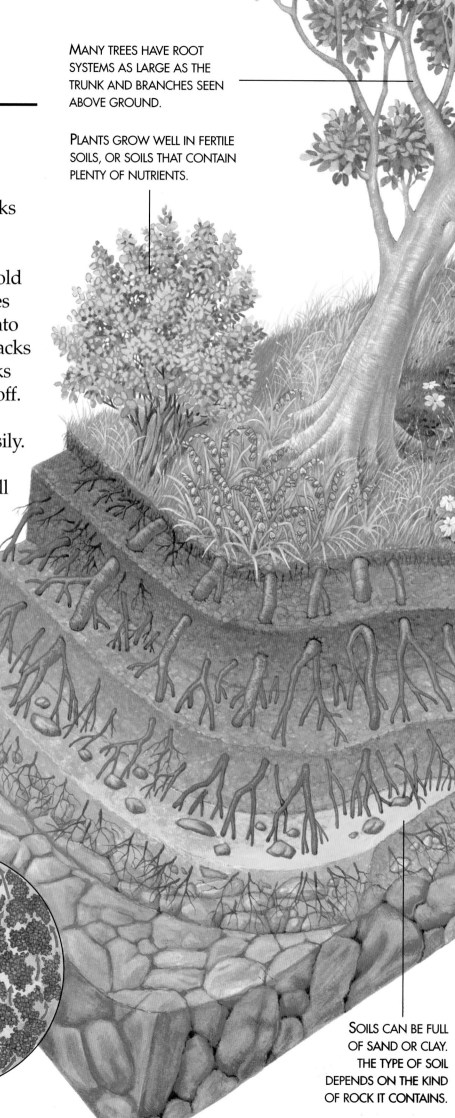

Soil is made of small pieces of rock and the decayed remains of dead organisms. It takes thousands of years for natural processes to break rocks into the small pieces that make up soil. Near the surface of Earth, the heat of summer makes rocks expand, and the cold of winter makes them shrink. This causes rocks to crack. Rainwater then trickles into the cracks. In winter, the water in the cracks freezes and expands, widening the cracks and causing fragments of rock to break off. Acids in the water also weaken rocks, which makes them break apart more easily. Rocks located deep underground are weakened by water in the soil. We call all the processes that help make soil by breaking up rocks "weathering."

MANY TREES HAVE ROOT SYSTEMS AS LARGE AS THE TRUNK AND BRANCHES SEEN ABOVE GROUND.

PLANTS GROW WELL IN FERTILE SOILS, OR SOILS THAT CONTAIN PLENTY OF NUTRIENTS.

MOST SOILS FORM AS DISTINCT LAYERS, ONE LYING ABOVE THE OTHER.

WATER MOVES BETWEEN THE PARTICLES OF SOIL.

Water in soil

Rainwater starts at the surface of the soil and moves downward between rock particles until it can go no farther. This water under the ground is called groundwater, and its upper surface is called the water table. As water on the surface of the soil evaporates into the air, it is replaced by groundwater, which is drawn upward through very small spaces. This upward movement of water keeps the soil moist.

SOILS CAN BE FULL OF SAND OR CLAY. THE TYPE OF SOIL DEPENDS ON THE KIND OF ROCK IT CONTAINS.

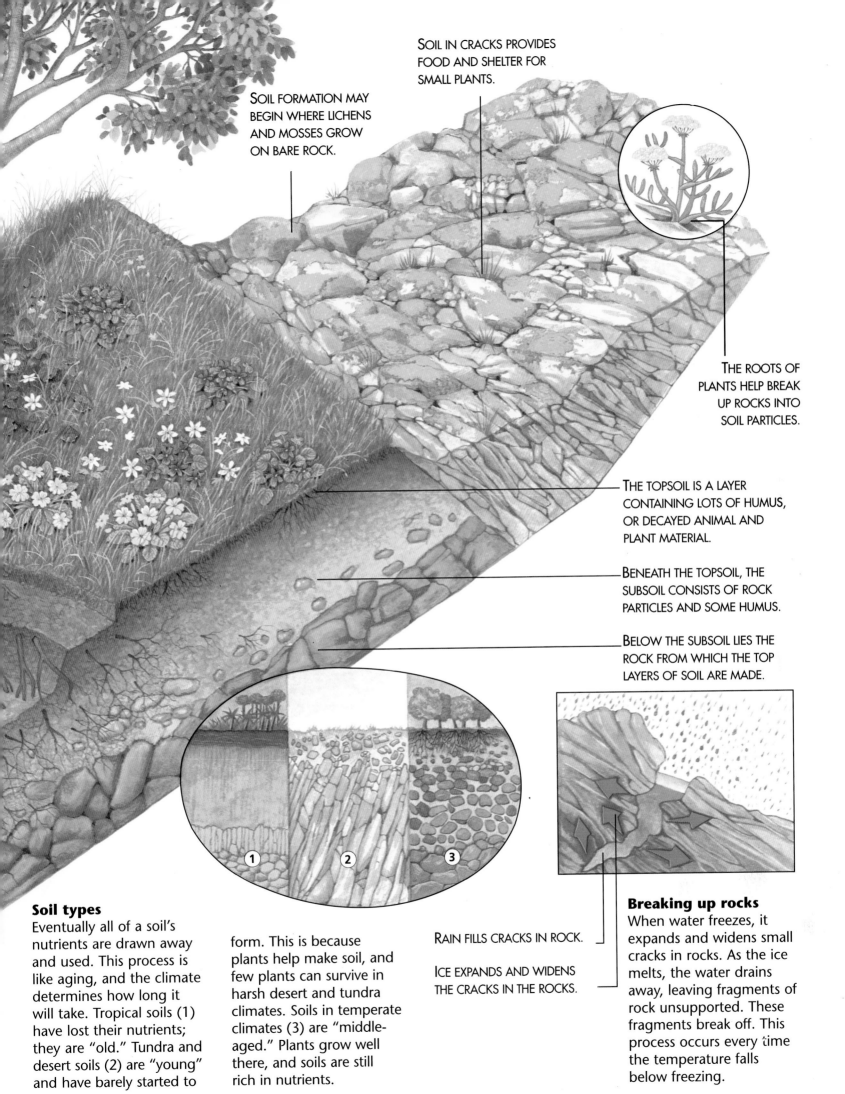

SOIL IN CRACKS PROVIDES
FOOD AND SHELTER FOR
SMALL PLANTS.

SOIL FORMATION MAY
BEGIN WHERE LICHENS
AND MOSSES GROW
ON BARE ROCK.

THE ROOTS OF
PLANTS HELP BREAK
UP ROCKS INTO
SOIL PARTICLES.

THE TOPSOIL IS A LAYER
CONTAINING LOTS OF HUMUS,
OR DECAYED ANIMAL AND
PLANT MATERIAL.

BENEATH THE TOPSOIL, THE
SUBSOIL CONSISTS OF ROCK
PARTICLES AND SOME HUMUS.

BELOW THE SUBSOIL LIES THE
ROCK FROM WHICH THE TOP
LAYERS OF SOIL ARE MADE.

Soil types

Eventually all of a soil's nutrients are drawn away and used. This process is like aging, and the climate determines how long it will take. Tropical soils (1) have lost their nutrients; they are "old." Tundra and desert soils (2) are "young" and have barely started to form. This is because plants help make soil, and few plants can survive in harsh desert and tundra climates. Soils in temperate climates (3) are "middle-aged." Plants grow well there, and soils are still rich in nutrients.

RAIN FILLS CRACKS IN ROCK.

ICE EXPANDS AND WIDENS
THE CRACKS IN THE ROCKS.

Breaking up rocks

When water freezes, it expands and widens small cracks in rocks. As the ice melts, the water drains away, leaving fragments of rock unsupported. These fragments break off. This process occurs every time the temperature falls below freezing.

Soil Life

Organisms living in the top few inches (cm) of soil in a field of grass may weigh more than the cows grazing in that field. Fertile soil is full of living organisms, from single-celled bacteria to animals the size of moles. Each organism occupies its own niche within the soil ecosystem. Woodlice, for example, eat decaying plant matter, and their droppings provide small pieces of simpler food for smaller organisms.

By living in or on the surface of the soil, organisms actually help make more soil. They do this by eating and breaking down, or decomposing, dead plant and animal materials.

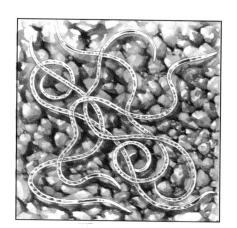

Nematodes

A vast number of nematodes, or eelworms, live in soil. Several millions of them may live in the first 4 inches (10 cm) of one square yard (1 sq. meter) of woodland soil. Nematodes look like microscopic threads (see above). The largest are barely .08 inches (2 mm) long. They live in water in the soil and eat plant roots, fungi, or bacteria. Nematodes help control the soil's population of microscopic organisms.

Mites

There are more mites than any other type of soil animal. Mites are tiny relatives of spiders. Plant-eating mites break leaves into smaller pieces (see below). Other mites hunt tiny animals.

FUNGI BREAK DOWN WOOD.

A SPIDER HUNTS FOR LICE.

EARTHWORMS INCH TOWARD THE SURFACE AT NIGHT TO DEPOSIT THEIR CASTS, OR WASTE MATTER.

WORM TUNNELS CREATE ROOM FOR AIR TO CIRCULATE IN SOIL.

THE MOLE DIGS LONG TUNNELS AND EATS THE WORMS AND OTHER ANIMALS THAT FALL INTO THEM.

A NEMATODE

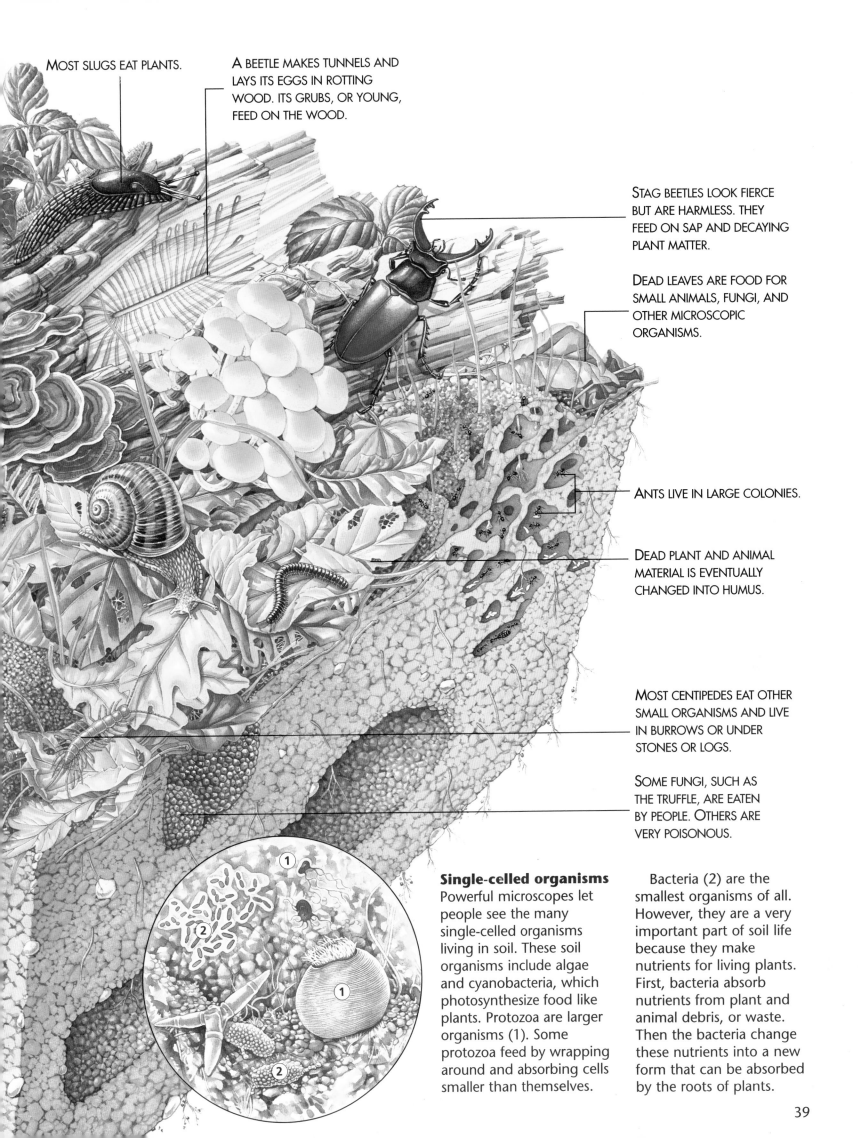

MOST SLUGS EAT PLANTS.

A BEETLE MAKES TUNNELS AND LAYS ITS EGGS IN ROTTING WOOD. ITS GRUBS, OR YOUNG, FEED ON THE WOOD.

STAG BEETLES LOOK FIERCE BUT ARE HARMLESS. THEY FEED ON SAP AND DECAYING PLANT MATTER.

DEAD LEAVES ARE FOOD FOR SMALL ANIMALS, FUNGI, AND OTHER MICROSCOPIC ORGANISMS.

ANTS LIVE IN LARGE COLONIES.

DEAD PLANT AND ANIMAL MATERIAL IS EVENTUALLY CHANGED INTO HUMUS.

MOST CENTIPEDES EAT OTHER SMALL ORGANISMS AND LIVE IN BURROWS OR UNDER STONES OR LOGS.

SOME FUNGI, SUCH AS THE TRUFFLE, ARE EATEN BY PEOPLE. OTHERS ARE VERY POISONOUS.

Single-celled organisms

Powerful microscopes let people see the many single-celled organisms living in soil. These soil organisms include algae and cyanobacteria, which photosynthesize food like plants. Protozoa are larger organisms (1). Some protozoa feed by wrapping around and absorbing cells smaller than themselves.

Bacteria (2) are the smallest organisms of all. However, they are a very important part of soil life because they make nutrients for living plants. First, bacteria absorb nutrients from plant and animal debris, or waste. Then the bacteria change these nutrients into a new form that can be absorbed by the roots of plants.

Rivers

When rainwater falls on bare rock or thin soil, it flows downhill across the surface of the land. If the soil is deep, the rainwater first seeps down until it meets rock. Then the water flows downhill. This underground water is called groundwater. In hollows, where rocks are closer to the surface, groundwater runs out as a spring.

On the surface of land, water flows in channels. A small channel of water is called a stream. Water constantly wears away at a stream, making it deeper. As more water flows from higher ground or from springs into a stream, the stream grows into a river. A river is home to many plants and animals. They live in distinct zones, which are called the headwaters, the troutbeck, the minnow zone, the bream zone, and the estuary.

Minnow zone

The river slows as it leaves the hills. Sediment, or mud, collects on its stony bottom, and plants take root in the mud. This is the minnow, or grayling, zone. Minnows and graylings feed on small animals, such as young fish and insects.

PLANTS SUCH AS THESE TAKE ROOT IN THE RIVER SEDIMENT.

ON ALMOST LEVEL GROUND, THE RIVER MEANDERS, WHICH MEANS THAT ITS PATH TWISTS FROM SIDE TO SIDE.

THE LAND IS NEARLY FLAT HERE. THIS AREA IS CALLED THE FLOOD PLAIN.

THE RIVER FLOWS OUT TO SEA.

Estuary zone

An estuary is where a river widens and meets a sea. The incoming tide brings salty seawater upstream. Where seawater and river water mix, small particles of soil sink and form banks of mud. The sea may also deposit sand. Worms and other small animals feed in the mud. They, in turn, are food for wading birds. The heron hunts for fish in shallow water *(see below)*.

SEDIMENT BUILDS UP INTO A MUD BANK.

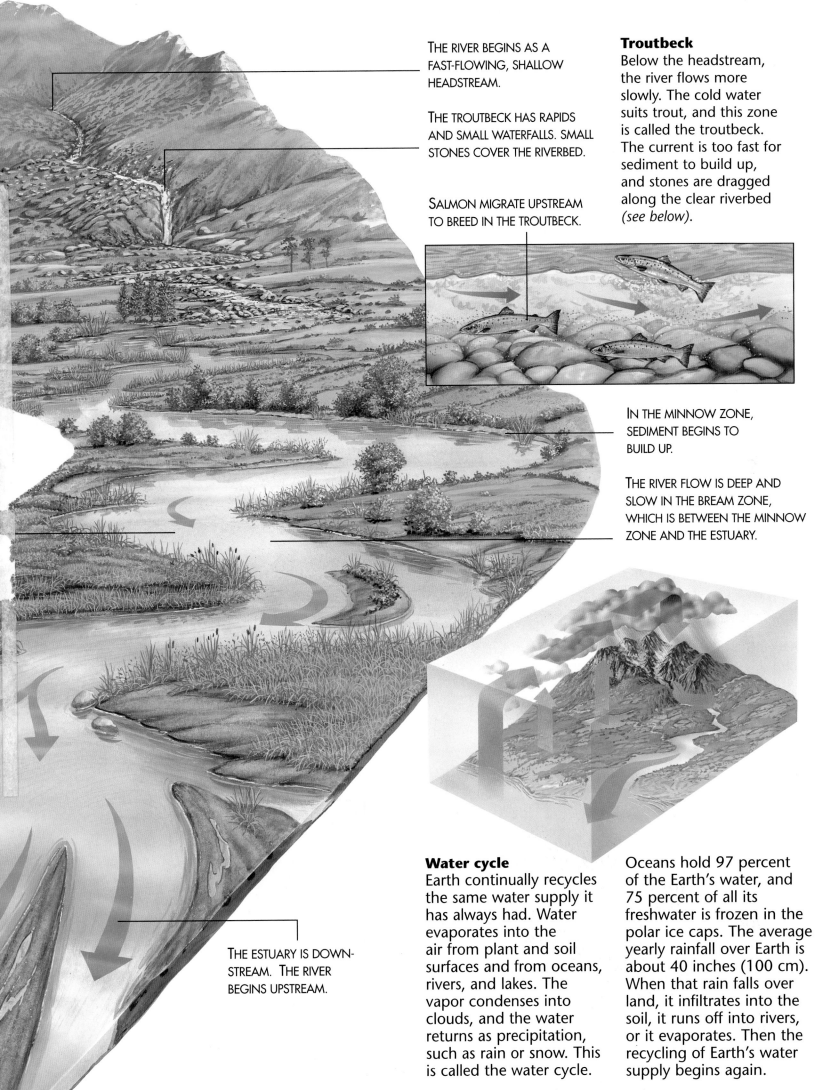

THE RIVER BEGINS AS A FAST-FLOWING, SHALLOW HEADSTREAM.

THE TROUTBECK HAS RAPIDS AND SMALL WATERFALLS. SMALL STONES COVER THE RIVERBED.

SALMON MIGRATE UPSTREAM TO BREED IN THE TROUTBECK.

Troutbeck
Below the headstream, the river flows more slowly. The cold water suits trout, and this zone is called the troutbeck. The current is too fast for sediment to build up, and stones are dragged along the clear riverbed *(see below)*.

IN THE MINNOW ZONE, SEDIMENT BEGINS TO BUILD UP.

THE RIVER FLOW IS DEEP AND SLOW IN THE BREAM ZONE, WHICH IS BETWEEN THE MINNOW ZONE AND THE ESTUARY.

THE ESTUARY IS DOWN-STREAM. THE RIVER BEGINS UPSTREAM.

Water cycle
Earth continually recycles the same water supply it has always had. Water evaporates into the air from plant and soil surfaces and from oceans, rivers, and lakes. The vapor condenses into clouds, and the water returns as precipitation, such as rain or snow. This is called the water cycle.

Oceans hold 97 percent of the Earth's water, and 75 percent of all its freshwater is frozen in the polar ice caps. The average yearly rainfall over Earth is about 40 inches (100 cm). When that rain falls over land, it infiltrates into the soil, it runs off into rivers, or it evaporates. Then the recycling of Earth's water supply begins again.

Environmental Damage

Humans cannot avoid changing the environment. Many of the changes are beneficial. However, there are also many human activities that harm the environment. Clearing rain forests or other natural vegetation to make farmland shrinks animal and plant habitats. Plants and animals are then confined to smaller and smaller areas. When their habitats are destroyed, some species die out completely. Waste products from homes and factories can pollute the air, oceans, and rivers. Pollution can poison organisms directly or indirectly by damaging their environment.

ABOUT 54,040 SQUARE MILES (140,000 SQ. KILOMETERS) OF TROPICAL RAIN FOREST ARE CLEARED EACH YEAR. THIS AREA IS BIGGER THAN GERMANY.

TRADITIONAL FARMERS FELL TREES AND BURN THE VEGETATION THEY CANNOT USE.

FOREST IS CLEARED TO ALLOW MINING FOR MINERALS.

Nowhere to live

Golden lion tamarins are tree-dwellers in the tropical forests of South America. When trees are cut down, tamarins have nowhere to live. Fewer than 300 wild tamarins are left. The species may soon be extinct.

ONCE ROADS ARE BUILT, FARMERS MOVE INTO THE FOREST AND CLEAR THE LAND TO GROW CROPS.

RAIN FOREST SOIL IS POOR, AND CROPS CAN FAIL.

IN SOME PLACES, CLEARED FOREST GROUND BECOMES AS HARD AS CONCRETE.

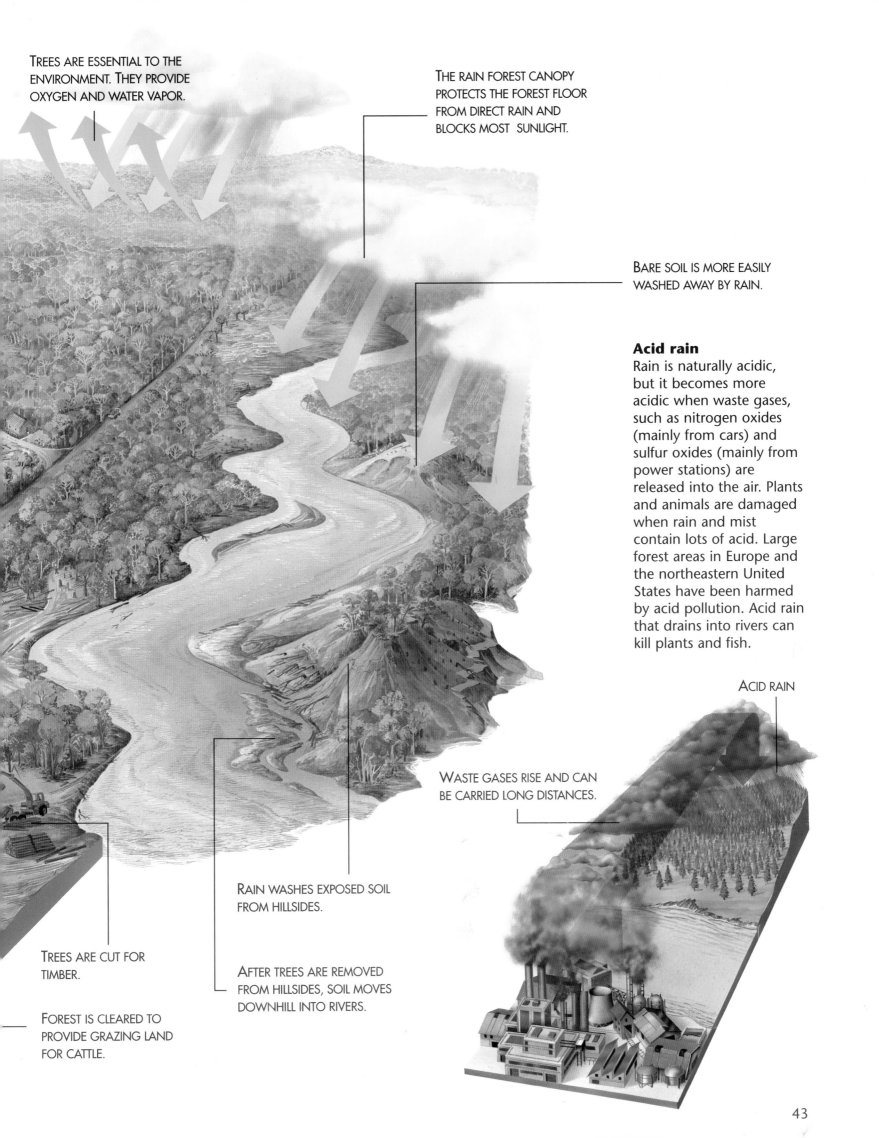

TREES ARE ESSENTIAL TO THE ENVIRONMENT. THEY PROVIDE OXYGEN AND WATER VAPOR.

THE RAIN FOREST CANOPY PROTECTS THE FOREST FLOOR FROM DIRECT RAIN AND BLOCKS MOST SUNLIGHT.

BARE SOIL IS MORE EASILY WASHED AWAY BY RAIN.

Acid rain

Rain is naturally acidic, but it becomes more acidic when waste gases, such as nitrogen oxides (mainly from cars) and sulfur oxides (mainly from power stations) are released into the air. Plants and animals are damaged when rain and mist contain lots of acid. Large forest areas in Europe and the northeastern United States have been harmed by acid pollution. Acid rain that drains into rivers can kill plants and fish.

ACID RAIN

WASTE GASES RISE AND CAN BE CARRIED LONG DISTANCES.

RAIN WASHES EXPOSED SOIL FROM HILLSIDES.

TREES ARE CUT FOR TIMBER.

AFTER TREES ARE REMOVED FROM HILLSIDES, SOIL MOVES DOWNHILL INTO RIVERS.

FOREST IS CLEARED TO PROVIDE GRAZING LAND FOR CATTLE.

Learning to Live in Harmony

Today most large industrial companies try to cause as little environmental damage as possible. Many companies are working to restore areas that, in the past, were damaged by pollution.

Mines, such as the china clay mine (*below*), can destroy wildlife and produce large piles of waste. For every ton of china clay mined, 9 tons (8 metric tons) of waste are produced. However, even the waste can be turned into green hills. Once mining is finished, the whole area can be restored or made into a golf course or community area. The hills may become grazing land for sheep. The illustrations on these pages show how this is done.

GRASS AND OTHER PLANT SEEDS ARE MIXED INTO WATER AND SPRAYED ONTO THE TERRACED SOIL.

ON THE SLOPES, THE WASTE IS SHAPED INTO LONG, FLAT TERRACES, OR STEPS.

RESTORATION OF THE LAND BEGINS AS SOON AS THE MINING IS FINISHED.

AS THE CLAY IS MINED, WASTE IS PILED UP TO FORM UGLY PYRAMIDS.

CHINA CLAY HAS MANY USES. THE PAPER IN THIS BOOK, FOR EXAMPLE, CONTAINS CHINA CLAY.

MINERS DIG A HUGE PIT SO THEY CAN REACH THE CLAY.

CLAY IS WASHED AWAY FROM ROCK WITH HIGH-PRESSURE WATER HOSES.

Polluted rivers
In the past, waste from the mine escaped into nearby rivers, coloring them white (1). With modern management, wastes are held back, and the rivers are their natural colors again (2).

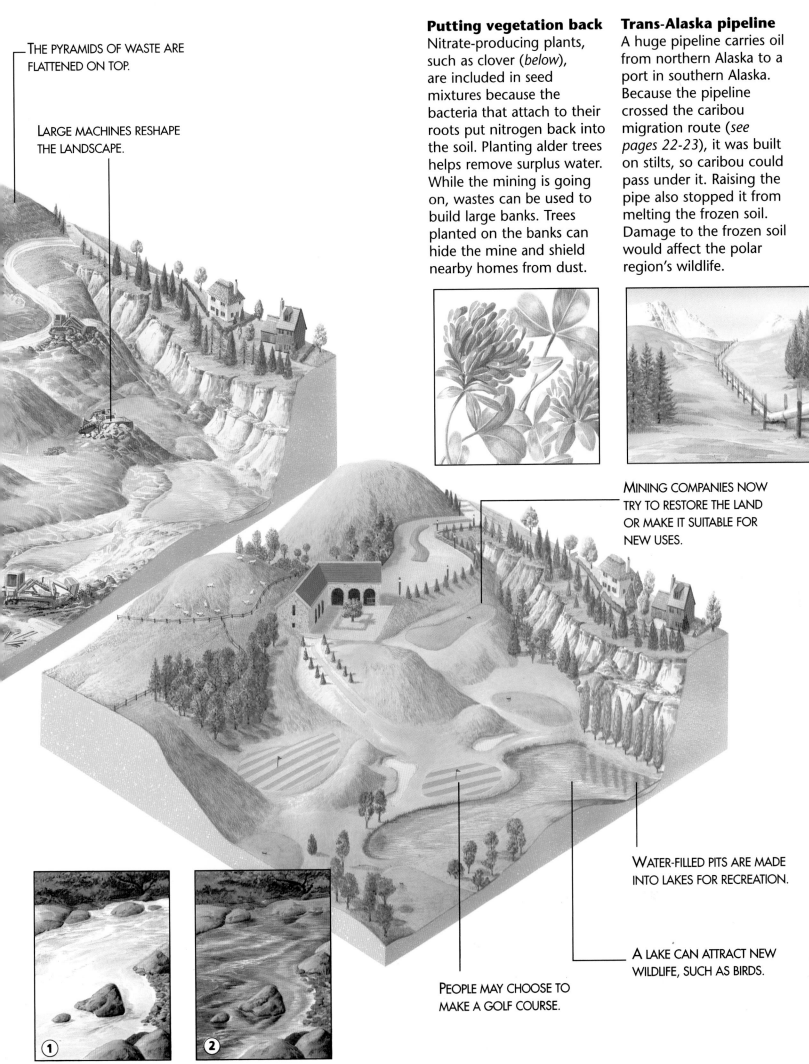

THE PYRAMIDS OF WASTE ARE FLATTENED ON TOP.

LARGE MACHINES RESHAPE THE LANDSCAPE.

Putting vegetation back

Nitrate-producing plants, such as clover (*below*), are included in seed mixtures because the bacteria that attach to their roots put nitrogen back into the soil. Planting alder trees helps remove surplus water. While the mining is going on, wastes can be used to build large banks. Trees planted on the banks can hide the mine and shield nearby homes from dust.

Trans-Alaska pipeline

A huge pipeline carries oil from northern Alaska to a port in southern Alaska. Because the pipeline crossed the caribou migration route (*see pages 22-23*), it was built on stilts, so caribou could pass under it. Raising the pipe also stopped it from melting the frozen soil. Damage to the frozen soil would affect the polar region's wildlife.

MINING COMPANIES NOW TRY TO RESTORE THE LAND OR MAKE IT SUITABLE FOR NEW USES.

WATER-FILLED PITS ARE MADE INTO LAKES FOR RECREATION.

A LAKE CAN ATTRACT NEW WILDLIFE, SUCH AS BIRDS.

PEOPLE MAY CHOOSE TO MAKE A GOLF COURSE.

① ②

Glossary

Antarctica: the frozen desert continent that surrounds the South Pole.

atmosphere: the layer of gases above Earth's crust that surrounds and protects Earth's surface.

auroras: colorful bands of light seen at night in the upper atmosphere of polar regions.

biome: a specific type of ecological community.

canopy: the thick layer of treetops in a rain forest.

carnivore: an animal that eats only meat.

cast: excreted earthworm waste.

chlorophyll: a green plant chemical that absorbs energy from sunlight. Without chlorophyll, plants could not make food from sunlight.

climate: the range of temperature, rainfall, and wind conditions found in a certain area.

core: the center of Earth; the inner core is made of solid metal, and the outer core is made of molten metal.

crust: Earth's outer layer that is only 3 to 37 miles (5 to 60 km) thick. People live on this thin crust.

current: the path and force of a stream of flowing water. Ocean currents can be warm or cold.

decompose: to break down or rot.

ecosystem: a community of plants and animals that lives together and draws on the food and energy sources of their shared surroundings.

equator: an imaginary line around the center of Earth. The equator divides Earth into a northern and a southern hemisphere.

estuary: the place where a river widens and meets the ocean so that salt- and freshwater mix.

flood plain: flat area of land that surrounds a river.

fossils: the remains or traces of plants and animals from an earlier time period.

gall: a round swelling that is caused by bacteria, insects, or fungi on a plant.

greenhouse gases: gases, such as carbon dioxide and nitrous oxide, that hold in heat that would otherwise escape into outer space.

gyre: an ocean current that flows in a circular path.

habitat: the type of place where an animal or plant naturally lives and grows.

herbivore: an animal that eats only plants.

humus: rich soil formed by dead leaves and other decomposed material.

krill: tiny, shrimp-like ocean creatures.

mantle: the middle layer of Earth. Large rocks and lava make up the mantle.

meander: to wind or twist gently or slowly.

meteor: a chunk of rock that burns up falling through Earth's atmosphere from outer space.

migrate: to move regularly from one area to another area; many animals migrate from cold climates to warm climates in winter.

omnivore: an animal that eats both plant and animal foods.

ozone: a special kind of oxygen in the atmosphere that blocks the Sun's harmful rays.

parasite: a plant or animal that survives by living or feeding on another plant or animal.

photosynthesis: a process in which plants use sunlight to combine water with carbon dioxide to produce sugars and oxygen.

phytoplankton: microscopic plants that float in the ocean and use sunlight for photosynthesis.

plate: in geology, a huge piece of slowly moving upper mantle rock and crust.

prey: animals that are hunted and eaten by other meat-eating animals.

respiration: the process by which plants and animals breathe. Oxygen is taken in and carbon dioxide is released during respiration.

sediment: sand, stones, and mud that build up in bodies of water.

tundra: an arctic or subarctic region where dense shrubs and herbs grow, but no trees.

weathering: the process of breaking large rocks into little fragments.

More Books to Read

The Automobile and the Environment. Earth at Risk (series). Maxine Rock (Chelsea House Publications)

Back to the Wild. Dorothy Hinshaw Patent and William Munoz (Gulliver Books)

Children's Atlas of the Environment. (Rand McNally)

Earth Book for Kids: Activities to Help Heal the Environment. Linda Schwartz and Beverly Armstrong (Learning Works)

The Encyclopedia of the Environment. Watts Encyclopedia Series. Stephen R. Kellert and Matthew Black (Franklin Watts)

Global Warming (SOS Earth Alert). Jean F. Blashfield and Wallace B. Black (Children's Press)

1001 Ideas for Science Projects on the Environment. Marion A. Brisk (Prentice Hall)

Science Fair Projects: The Environment. Dan Keen, Bob Bonnet, Robert L. Bonnet, and Frances Zweifel (Sterling Publications)

The Talking Earth. Jean Craighead George (HarperCollins)

What You Can Do for the Environment. Mike Wald (Chelsea House Publications)

Working in the Environment. Exploring Careers (series). Corinna Nelson (Lerner Publications)

Videos

Life on Earth. (Warner Home Video)

National Geographic's Rain Forest. (National Geographic)

Private Life of Plants. (Turner Home Entertainment)

Trials of Life Collection. (Turner Home Entertainment)

Web Sites

Children of the Earth United
www.childrenoftheearth.org/

Earth Day Network
www.earthday.net/

The Environment: A Global Challenge
library.thinkquest.org/26026/

Environment On-line
solstice.crest.org/environment/eol/toc.html

Global Warming: Focus on the Future
www.enviroweb.org/edf/

NASA's Earth Observatory
earthobservatory.nasa.gov/

The Ozone Hole Tour
www.atm.ch.cam.ac.uk/tour/index.html

U.S. EPA Explorers Club
www.epa.gov/kids/

Some web sites stay current longer than others. For additional web sites, use reliable search engines to locate the following topics: *biomes, environment, food web, greenhouse effect, migration, ozone layer,* and *pollution*.

Index